THE ORATORIOS OF HANDEL

By the same author :

SAMUEL PEPYS MUSIC BOOK

PAGEANT OF ENGLAND'S MUSIC

HANDEL

MUSIC IS FOR YOU

MENDELSSOHN

Handel—from a portrait by Kneller (after 1750)

THE
ORATORIOS
OF
HANDEL

BY PERCY M. YOUNG

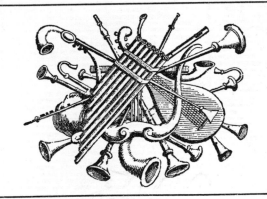

LONDON

PUBLISHED BY DENNIS DOBSON LTD

First published in Great Britain in MCMXLIX by
DENNIS DOBSON LIMITED, 12 Park Place, St James's,
London SW1. All rights reserved. Printed in Great Britain
by PAGE BROS (NORWICH) LTD.
133/R

CONTENTS

LIST OF ILLUSTRATIONS

INTRODUCTION

THERE are two reasons for the writing of this book. On the one hand is the conviction that the works discussed herein represent one of the chief glories of musical achievement: on the other the opinion that they should be conspicuous among our musical endeavours. We are, in England, in danger of losing our choral excellence by general concentration on a handful of well-tried 'favourite' works and by an excessive affection for large orchestras and large choirs which, in occasional conjunction, frequently make a great deal of noise. Choral singing, again speaking in general terms and without reflection on a few choirs which achieve eminence, suffers a lack of subtlety and too often is synonymous with community singing. The corrective to this is a course in Handel, whose understanding of choral values can only be appreciated when his voice parts are treated with the respect accorded by the best orchestral musicians to the music which they play.

Handel's oratorios stand for more than artistic genius. They form an anthology of variations on aspects of English life which, we may like to think, typify our individual humane tradition. We discover a love of simple beauty, an inclination to the picturesque, a sensitivity to words, a practical approach to problems of religion and a concern for the welfare of men and women: men and women rather than the aggregation more pompously termed mankind. The age of Handel and the music of Handel, which reflects the age, can teach us much about the art of living, both singly and in community. By taking part in music such as this and by

9

taking pains in preparation we may, perhaps, learn more of the nature of democracy than from all the preachers. This is social music and encourages fraternity. It is great music practicable for all who are adventurous and willing to learn to sing at sight.

The depth of Handel does not become apparent from a perfunctory *Messiah*, hardly rehearsed because 'we have done it before' but only from excursions among the other oratorios. It is true that pioneer work in resuscitating the forgotten oratorios (and operas) has been done and we should be grateful. But these efforts make little impression on those who so often justify their allegiance to Handel by indifference to most of his output. My concern is for the choral singers who still abound and still remain the principal evidence for a modest claim that we are not an unmusical race. By experience I know that singing Handel other than *Messiah* can stimulate, enthrall, and entertain amateur singers. In the hope that historical and critical discussion of the oratorios may widen practical interest this book is put forth. Biography is mostly avoided since I have dealt with that elsewhere. So too are the secular oratorios, which are more advantageously studied away from the 'sacred' associations of the works discussed herein. I shall hope to deal with them on another occasion.

The assistance of the following is gratefully acknowledged: those authorities in Wolverhampton and Staffordshire, whose substantial sympathy has made possible various performances, without which the book would have lacked conviction; my singers and the Riddick orchestra for their imaginative insight and loyal co-operation; Professor G. H. P. Hewson and the Dean of St Patrick's Cathedral, Dublin; Mr John Russell of the Henry Watson Music Library in Manchester; Mr E. H. Dance; Miss M. E. Gayler; Mr Eric Greene; and, finally, the authorities noted within for their courtesy in permitting the illustrations to appear.
Wolverhampton, 15 February, 1948   P.M.Y.

Chapter One

ITALIAN ORIGINS

I N art, as in nature, nothing can ever be said to have a beginning. Therefore the slide-rule of the historian which marks the year 1600 as an *annus mirabilis* in the development both of opera and oratorio should be treated with discretion. It is true that Cavalieri's *L'anima e corpo* and Peri's *Euridice* were heard—the one in Rome, the other in Florence—in that year, but the facts need perspective. Statistics assume significance only when related to the human interests which they symbolize. Music, and indeed all art, must be related to the society for which and by which it is created. Abstract theories regarding art rarely produce works of art (the theoretical origins of opera in particular tend to distort the vision because they receive emphasis at the expense of human values of relevance). Therefore we would preface this study of oratorio with a Chesterton epigram: 'Nothing sublimely artistic has ever arisen out of mere art'.

That Italy proved such fertile ground for the nourishment of seeds which were to burst into flower at the touch of Scarlatti and Handel, was because of particular reasons, at least half of which are not directly musical. One inescapable fundamental and musical factor, however, persists. The Italians were (and are) singers. This truism may be amplified to demonstrate its singularity. The Italians sing not so much

11

because they want to, but because they must, and their singing permeates the whole of life. Goldoni writes of the Venetians—'Everyone sings, on the squares, in the streets, on the canals. The merchants sing when they are selling, the workers going to their tasks, the gondoliers waiting for their masters.' Burney records this of Florence.

The historian Villani, contemporary with Petrarca, says that his *canzoni* were universally sung in Florence, by the old and the young of both sexes. And historians relate that *Lorenzo il Magnifico*, in Carnival time, used to go out in the evening, followed by a numerous company of persons on horseback, masked, and richly dressed, amounting sometimes upwards of three hundred; and the same number on foot, with wax tapers burning in their hands. In this manner they marched through the city, till three or four o'clock in the morning, singing songs, ballads, madrigals, catches, or songs of humour upon subjects then in vogue, with *musical harmony*, in four, eight, twelve, and even fifteen parts, accompanied with various instruments; and these, from being performed in Carnival time, were called *Canti Carnascialeschi*.

While Burney himself was in Florence he noted that in such traditions there is little change from century to century.

But even before this period the company of *Laudisti* or Psalm-singers was formed, which has continued ever since; it is now called *La Compagnia*, and the morning after my arrival in Florence, between six and seven o'clock, they passed by the inn where I lodged, in grand procession, dressed in a whitish uniform, with burning tapers in their hands. They stopped at the *duomo*, or great church, just by, to sing a chearful hymn, in three parts, which they executed very well. In this manner, on Sundays and holidays, the trades-people and artizans form themselves into distinct companies, and sing through the streets, in their way to church. Those of the parish of S. Benedetto, we are informed by Crescimbeni, were famous all over Italy; and at the great Jubilee, in the beginning of this century, marched through the streets of Rome, singing in such a manner as pleased and astonished every body.

We see on the common level the interfusion of music and religion, which was the basis of Italian oratorio. But the direction which singing, and music in general, was to take was pointed by historical phenomena. Three of these, not without parallel in more recent times, were particularly significant to sixteenth century Italy.

The interventionist powers of France, Spain, and the Empire treated the Italian countryside as an ideal ground for testing their strength in military prowess and dynastic ambition. The French, for example, fought one campaign after another from the reign of Charles VIII to that of Henri II. Since there was no Italian nation, but merely a collection of feudal states, this gave an unhealthy stimulus to internecine warfare and to spiteful essays in depredation. Under such conditions the sensitive citizen either turns to cynicism for cold and bitter comfort or he endeavours to safeguard his spiritual integrity by devoting himself to spiritual and intellectual exercise. So much for the private citizen. The people of Italy were thrown unconsciously into the field of aspirant nationalism by their dependence on the outcome of political chicanery, of the intermittent hostilities between alien powers, by the lesser annoyances of ambitious popes, priests, and princelings. But nationalism was not politically conscious; its expression was through literature, architecture, art, music, and a revitalized religion. It is no fantasy to conclude that out of adversity comes good, though the process may not seem attractive to the victim. It may be said that the 'definitive consolidation of the literary Italian language', without which there would have been no dramatic resurgence and, consequently, no libretti for opera and oratorio, came through a natural though subconscious desire to show to France and Spain that part of Italy which was inviolable. Developments in language were influential elsewhere and we later discover the spontaneity and vigorous colour contrasts of the painter Caravaggio.

Politics had two main centres, the secular and the religious. It would be incorrect to assume that the greatest political gesture of religious history—the Reformation— was without meaning to Italy. Italy was affected as were other parts of Europe, but in a different way. Popular

B

protestantism was as impracticable under the double totali-
tarianism of Spain and the Papacy as ever was democracy in
a rigorously regimented Fascist state. The English have a
vague impression even now of the character of that most
'Christian' ruler, Philip II. For the independently inclined
religious thinker there were varied disciplinary prospects:
the policy of heretical extirpation, in which Pope Pius V
displayed remarkable zeal; the Inquisitorial *auto de fé*, the
corpus juris canonicis, the Index and the rest of a relentless
machinery. The mills of God's Italian lieutenants were
accustomed throughout the sixteenth century to grind not
too slowly, but exceedingly small.

Part of the ecclesiastical machinery was operated by the
religious orders, the revivification of which was one of the
notable features of sixteenth century life. The Catholic
church can rarely be accused of lack of catholicity and two
organizations in particular illustrate the wide possibilities
open to those seeking the religious life. At the one extreme
there was the Society of Jesus, wherein was regimentation:
at the other was the fraternity grouped round St Philip Neri.
In this society one senses a humane, even a libertarian
influence. Our story may conveniently start with St Philip
(even though, in truth, it cannot—*a priori*—start).

It was not for nothing that St Philip became rapidly
among the most cultivated of saints. As a matter of interest
and perhaps of relevence we find the traveller de Bainville
writing, in the year in which Handel set out for Italy, 'The
Devotion paid to St *Philip Neri*, tho' so modern a Saint, and
the Confidence which the People put in him, throughout
all parts of *Italy*, are almost incredible. Few Miracles are
wrought in this Country, in which he has not a share.' He
possessed, to a rare degree, a combination of natural and
supernatural excellence. He was amiable, imaginative,
efficient, and pious. We may meet his likeness in an evidently
truthful, if somewhat idealized, portrait by Pomarancio. A
keen, straight vision looks out from the canvas. A high,

intellectual forehead and a misshapen nose suggest sensitive and scholarly inclinations together with an affection for virile and athletic diversion. The mouth, above a patriarchal beard, is not far from laughter. If we were to choose our father confessor from a portrait gallery, St Philip Neri would be a ready choice. Pomarancio's portraiture speaks more directly and truthfully than the hagiolatrous miscellany on which otherwise we have to rely. The morals of musicians being notorious to those who are not musicians, we may write, as posthumous testimonial, the list of those of the musical fraternity among his clients.

At the head of the list should be placed Giovanni Animuccia, who succeeded Palestrina as *maestro di capella* at St Peter's in 1556. He joined the Oratory and persuaded his wife Lucrezia to entrust her spiritual direction to St Philip. Other notable female penitents to follow Lucrezia's example were Delia Buscaglia, wife of the instrumentalist Gaspare Brizzio and mother of Giovanni Francesca Brizzio; Bradamante, wife of Asprilio Pacelli and her sister Fulvia, who was married to Maurizio Anerio and whose son was Giovanni Francesco Anerio. A close relationship may be deduced between St Philip and the changing musical tradition of Rome.

We are still some way from oratorio as an art form, but the conditions which made it possible for oratorio to develop along the lines ultimately followed were partly created by the particular outlook of St Philip. He is less important, musically speaking, than is frequently indicated (the accidental association of oratorio and oratory is a too convenient *terminus a quo*) but much more significant when viewed from a musical-social angle. The oratorios of Handel are conspicuously secular works, but none the less they are religious as well. The renaissance of religious romanticism, that appreciation of consecrated secularity and even vulgarity, that acceptance of lively devoutness as a foil to the morbidity of disembodied dogma and discipline, came in the sixteenth century from St Philip Neri as in the thirteenth it had come from St Francis of Assisi. Handel's knowledge of Italy was of later date but the catholicity of Neri still persisted.

The essence of music is freedom (an orderly freedom let it be noted). The effect of music on narrative is to release poetry from the commonplace. St Philip had, broadly speaking, a musical philosophy, so that when preaching the doctrine of spiritual emancipation he found himself obliged to conscribe the arts.

There is a curious and charming anticipation, in the practice of the Oratorians, of the procedure of the Society of Friends. At afternoon sessions most of the time was 'devoted to discourses made in accordance with the inspiration which the Holy Spirit gave to each speaker'. After Vespers on Sundays and Feast Days it was the custom for St Philip to encourage pleasant relaxation. His 'medley of gentlemen and artisans, of educated men and simple folk', his growing circle of young disciples, and a varied assemblage of camp-followers would walk the pleasaunces of the Eternal City. To the Campagna, to the Janiculum, to the Baths of Diocletian: in some shady spot they would sit down to discuss contemporary problems of literature and music. The method of applying culture and of practising social welfare startled the conventional, but as a model for the enrichment of leisure St Philip's practice could hardly be bettered. At Easter there was a ceremonial pilgrimage to the Seven Churches and it is evident that this occasion borrowed from rites older than those of Christianity. The luxuriant thought of alfresco meals accompanied by the trumpeters of the Castle of St Angelo (Gaspare Brizzio and Maurizio Anerio were members both of that corporation and also of the Oratory) and attendant choristers introduces fragrant recollection of Floralia. In procession from church to church, the pilgrims were heartened by the singing of two choirs. What comprised this *tonus peregrinus* is not

known, but there may, quite reasonably, be associated with
it the names of Animuccia and Palestrina. At any rate the
processional music would not have been stylistically different from that which adorned the solemn mass at St
Sebastian or St Etienne, nor from that belonging to the
final service of the day, with its customary motet in honour
of the Blessed Virgin, at St Maria Maggiore.

The setting of these musical performances among the
friends of St Philip, sometimes in church and sometimes
beneath the vaster dome of a Roman sky removes the
association with dry-as-dust antiquity which possibly influences the approach of the contemporary listener to works of
that period.

The growth of music is gradual and imperceptible and
revolutions in development are rarer than is sometimes
thought. There may occur changes of direction, but as a
rule these follow from previous developments.

Opera is primarily an adjustment of musical to verbal
values. Before Peri and Cavalieri had startled their micro-
cosms with a form of recitative whose effectiveness cannot
be perceived through paper evidence (the discrepancies
between notation and performance must always be allowed
for in early music) Animuccia had explicitly indicated the
growing liaison between music and poetry in the introduction to his *Laudi* of 1570. That these were *ad hoc* works
for the Oratory is evident from their preamble and one may
detect in the technical apologia a reflection of congregational
discussion; for, as has already been indicated, Oratory
congregations were not averse from debate. 'It seemed',
wrote Animuccia, 'to be more suitable to the words themselves, to the nature of that place of devotion for which I
was composing, and to the end which I had in view, which
was only to excite devotion. But the aforesaid Oratory
having, by the grace of God, steadily grown by reason of
the concourse of prelates and the most distinguished
gentlemen, it has seemed proper to me in this second book

to develop the harmonies, repairing, as far as I can, from the complication of fugues and other devices so as not to obscure the sense of the words.' There is nothing like counterpoint for the achievement of verbal incoherence. So long as familiar texts from the Mass or from the Bible were involved, not hearing the words was of no great concern, but as soon as stimulating poetry by Jacopone da Todi was introduced to music (or themes from Ariosto or Tasso) it was important that they should be intelligible. The *Laudi* of Jacopone exercised great influence over the Oratorians: lyrical, picturesque, in part didactic, and frequently dramatic —the *Pianta della Madonna* is, as it stands, ripe for oratorio treatment by a Handel or a Pergolesi—they revealed an attractiveness in exegesis not lost on susceptible artistic sensibilities and pointed directly at nascent *dramma per musica*.

The disability under which Palestrina labours is respectability. The calm refinement of sequestered English church music tradition reads too much between the lines to be entirely truthful in its interpretation of Palestrina. The cathedral organist and director of the Julian choir is recollected at the expense of the other Palestrina. For the same man was a dabbler in real estate speculation, an uxorious refugee from holy orders, and a sycophant. A false estimate of the ecclesiastical style of the period disguises his innate love of richness, colour, and humour, qualities which ride high in such works as *The Song of Songs*. Palestrina may be a classic, but he was not conscious of the fact himself. One may expect that he could not have been indifferent to Baroque adventurousness.

Oratorio with which we are familiar involves choral participation and it is important to realize that backing this factor lay a wealth of dramatic emphasis; equally important is it to accept some relationship of outlook between the sixteenth and eighteenth centuries. Palestrina was in close touch with the Oratory. St Philip was, for a time at all events, his spiritual director, while Persiano Rosa, St Philip's confessor, and Angelo Vetti, a father of the Congregation, were natives of Palestrina. A further link is established through Fr Francisco Soto, a Spaniard, who published a set of *Laudi* employed at the Oratory. Among them were settings by Palestrina.

There is a great deal that we do not know of Palestrina. We do not know, although it seems a fair deduction, that he took part in aesthetic discussion at the Oratory; we do not precisely know the type of dramatic song there encouraged; we do not know what music Palestrina wrote for the orchestral ensemble of Hippolyte d'Este; nor do we know which of his works were sung out-of-doors. We do know that the academic point of view frequently deals with the bones of music. We should remember that Palestrina and his contemporaries were not without some concern for the flesh thereof.

That enthusiastic and informed student of Italian affairs, Vernon Lee, wrote:

The Italy of a century ago is interesting because, in a time of mere philosophic speculation, it alone created artistic form, not eclectic, but national and spontaneous; because to it belongs perhaps the last great artistic efflorescence, which was not, like that which produced Shelley and Keats, a reaction; nor like that which produced Goethe and Schiller, a revival; but was like the efflorescence of art to which we owe Phidias, Raphael, Dante, or Shakespeare, the culmination of a long and unbroken series of artistic phenomena.

With Palestrina and St Philip we are implicated in this series: with Handel we shall be somewhere near a point of culmination. In many ways we are made conscious of the earlier Italian tradition in Handel's style but there are less obvious points of contact. There is, for example, the attitude towards suitability. Here again we may refer to Vernon Lee.

The music performed in the churches was, as a rule, not very different from that performed in the theatres; for the fact is, that there never has existed such a thing as church music independent of the other branches of the art. There have been various styles of music, one belonging to each epoch, and which have been adapted, one after the other, to all the musical requirements of the time, the church, the theatre, or the room. . . . The style of the Roman school of the sixteenth century may possibly be more suitable for ecclesiastical purposes than any other . . . but it is undeniable that this style was the only one then extant, and that Palestrina himself set profane madrigals to that very sort of music which is held up as the only sort fit for the church.

Changes in technique and style came about, therefore, not through considerations of propriety but through the opportunities offered by various kinds of enlightened patronage. Thus, sometime before 1600, helped by Ottavio Rinuccini, incited by Bardi, Strozzi, and other 'learned and enlightened lovers of the fine arts' (with somewhat doctrinaire ideas), Peri produced *Ariadne*, and through adroit publicity drew credit for the invention of recitative.

The inevitable application of new operatic principles to music ancillary to religion (not 'religious' music) was given official recognition by its performance in the then unfinished church of St Maria at Valicella in Rome. The production was Emilio del Cavaliere's *L'anima e di corpo* with 'scenes, decorations, and acting chorus *à l'antique*, and dances'.

The generous breadth of Neri's vision must have infected his successors at St Maria (the church was made over to St Philip in 1575) for Cavaliere's work, despite a dull, medieval morality plot, had attractive accessories. The off-stage orchestra of lira doppia, clavicembalo, chitarone, and flutes was a common domestic ensemble, while the dances ranged from galliards to canaries, and from canaries to courants. (Dances *ad majorem dei gloriam* have their rightful place in the warmer traditions of southern and Catholic countries.) While the flippant may have been encouraged by such interpolations it is possible that the simple and devout knew something of the value of linking trivial with more formal tributes to the Almighty. Thus the Handel overture minuet has honourable ancestry, although he fell temporary victim to English puritan sentiment by the omission of this movement in the *Messiah* overture.

The crowds which jostled the Valicella did not make the mistake of overvaluing Cavaliere: only Cavaliere did that, and subsequent estimates of his worth have been obedient to his own valuation. His ideas on performance, however, are more interesting than those about himself This may be compared with later views on later singers.

. . . And a singer of such music is required by Cavaliere to have a fine voice, perfectly in tune, and free from all defects in the delivery of it; with a pathetic expression, the power of swelling and diminishing the tones, and an equal respect for the composer and the poet, in singing plain, and being particularly attentive to the articulation and expression of the words.

One fragment of chorus may be quoted as evidence of the vulgarity (to use the word literally) appreciated by the Oratorians. Forgetting the forbidding appearance of the notation (the white notes of ancient music are misleading) and remembering the terpsichorean lilt of the trochee, a light-hearted turn may be given to the study of oratorio.

Before we leave this particular work it may be mentioned that its ascription to the amateur Cavaliere is not beyond doubt. There is an alternative author in the person of Dionisio

Isorelli, another amateur, a lay brother of the Oratorians (1599) whose main concern was with their musical affairs.

That music has progressed (even if we only accept the indisputability of technical development) is symbolic of the spiritual urgency in human nature. The evolution of the *nuove musiche* was in spite of continual and distracting external difficulties. Oratorio, which is an integral part of seventeenth century artistic emancipation, must be set against a background not of idyllic languor but a wilder and vaster panorama of dirt, disease, murderous disputation, and social upheaval. During the century the sack of cities was commonplace: Mantua was ravaged by Imperial forces in 1630, in the middle of the century almost every central Italian city was spoliated by the War of Castro, severe rioting disturbed the Neapolitan scene in 1647, Venice continued practical enmity with the Turks for the space of twenty years, and Genoa suffered bombardment by the French in 1684. A little later Handel left Rome at the imminence of yet another of its periodic sieges. The easy humour of Italian society was more apparent than real. The philosophy of those who endured such variety of vicissitude was simple and classic: *carpe diem*. But to this there was another side. A potentially brief expectation of life led to an enjoyment of carnal pleasures, but it also stimulated visions of eternal life and these, in turn, were nourished by art and religion. The fullness of the classic musical tradition of Italy was caused in large measure by an awareness of the life beyond life.

Between Cavaliere and Carissimi, whose name is memorable if only because his *Jephthe* is easily available for examination and because his ideas helped to fertilize those of Handel, it is worth while turning to the testimony of Pietro della Valle, a commentator on the state of Roman music about the year 1640.

First as to style. The old masters 'were well acquainted

with harmony, but few knew what use to make of it',
while they were

> so far from thinking of the accent or expression of words, that they
> never chuse them till after the Music is composed, and then adapt the
> first they can find.

This is not the method by which modern masters proceed; they have
learned how to chuse and respect good poetry, in setting which they
relinquish all the pedantry of canons, fugues, and other Gothic
inventions; and, in imitation of the ancient Greeks, aspire at nothing
but expression, grace, and propriety.

Next as to singers. Nothing like the contemporary skill
had ever been heard before: this, of course, is an optative
fallacy repeated from generation to generation. At the same
time the soprano chorus of sirenical female and evirate male
had, in mid-century, an element of novelty. 'At present
every court and every chapel in Italy is furnished with them.'
Opera nurtured the singers and they the developing opera.
Oratorio was implicated as a cognate department of music
proceeding *pari passu*.

In 1644 Evelyn visited St Philip Neri's Chiesa Nuova.
'This evening [November 8] I was invited to heare rare
musiq at the Chiesa Nuova'; after a sermon and an oration,
the latter delivered by a child of eight or nine and much
applauded by Evelyn, '[they] began their Motettos, which, in
a lofty cupola richly painted, were sung by eunuchs and
other rare voices, accompanied with theorbos, harpsicors,
and viols, so that we were even ravish'd with the entertainment of the evening.' Clearly the era of the *castrati* was
begun. Of this tribe another, anonymous, member impressed
Evelyn when he heard the opera *Hercules in Lydia*. This
eunuch surpassed, so he said, the great Roman singer
Anna Rencia. By the side of the two sopranos, male and
female, Evelyn placed an incomparable bass—a Genoese.
Sopranos and basses were the idols of the day. Altos and
tenors were yet to come into their own. In the seventeenth
and eighteenth centuries both vocal and orchestral music
was largely a matter of top and bottom. The reason is not

far to seek. Melody supported by a well defined bass was all important. An attractive principle providing it is not regarded from the standpoint which considers the complexity of late German harmonic method essential. Once again this underlies the music of Handel which, in fair representation, should be freed from the fuller idiom of Mozart and the alien richness of the pianoforte.

The line of renaissance melody absorbed many influences —the reforming zeal of the *stilo recitativo* specialists did nothing to dispel the popular belief in the integrity of melodic spontaneity while singers saw to it that there was a sufficiency of composers to furnish them with fluent airs— and we learn from della Valle of the incursion into Rome of Neapolitan ballads, Sicilian, Spanish, Portuguese, and other foreign airs. It might also be remembered that Monteverde finished his *Orfeo* with a Moorish dance. The propinquity of music, commerce, scholarship, and warfare is by no means a negligible factor in historical review.

For the most part the oratorios and even the operas of the seventeenth century are dismissed today as containing only antiquarian interest and this province is conventionally handed to the governance of the academic. This is a minor tragedy because the endeavour to set antiquity in perspective instructs the imagination, and the general imagination is not so versatile that it can dispense with variety of exercise. The end of historical research is reached when personality, purpose, actions, and effect are integrated within the consciousness of the observer so that he too feels himself to be within the scene of his consideration.

Vernon Lee, with a similar point of view, commented, 'The impression comes home to us how deep an abyss separates us from the men and women for whom the plays were written and the music composed, and how many faint and nameless ghosts crowd round the few enduring things bequeathed to us by the past.' Handel produced some part of the few enduring things. Behind him, in point of time, were many ghosts who, if not without name, went unnoticed to their several graves. These posterity has left quietly to rest under the drums and tramplings of more than three conquests.

Michelagnolo Capollini, Michel Angelo Rossi, a violinist of high renown (for those were days in which composition was not a specialized department), Cavalier Loreto Vittorj, a soprano singer whose music may well have been among Evelyn's enchantments at the Chiesa Nuova (his published opera of *Galatea* also momentarily catches our interest), Mazzocchi, Landi, and Frederici were among the less known forerunners of the Handelian oratorio. From their achievement certain facts emerge. The Chiesa Nuova was persistent in promoting new music. The vogue for oratorio was widespread, from Venice to Messina. The cultivated among the churchmen were inclined to intellectual interest—Landi and Mazzocchi were patronized by the Florentine Barberini and by Aldobrandini Borghese. The tendency in presentation was towards the picturesque: lachrymose crucifixion scenas; abbreviated biographies of such attractive saints as Caterina da Sienne (though in Frederici's oratorio of this name (1676) an earlier moralistic influence obtrudes in the personified World, Vanity, and Repentance) and Philip Neri himself; the stock in trade of biblical fable—Samson, Deborah, Susanna (all Handelian subjects), Abraham, and Isaac, and the two Marys all provoked numerous settings. There are three subjects treated in this prolific period which might attract the attention, even now, of some potential oratorio composer in search of a theme—San Tommaso di Canturbia, Tommaso Moro, and Maria Stuardia, Regina di Scozia.

Landi, who has already received mention, deserves further consideration if only on account of his preface to *Il S. Alessio Dramma Musicale*. In this—such apologiae were not uncommon—Landi informs us 'that the ritornels for violins are in three parts; but that sometimes there is a base [sic] added to them which often moves in eighths and fifths with one of the parts, on purpose, for the *beauty of the effect*. After this declaration,' continues Burney, 'the musical reader will perhaps have as little eagerness to see such Music as I had to transcribe it, after examining the score.' Landi, however, would have had the last laugh. The stress, we learn from this statement, was on the exposition of emotional possibilities. Further evidence on this head comes from Mazzocchi who affected the dignified contrapuntal competence of the old school and at the same time added nuance to both the harmonic and the dynamic vocabulary. There is in Mazzocchi the expressive endeavour of individual style in suspensory discord, the colouring of generous modulation, and the new symbolism of < and >, which signs seem to appear for the first time in the music of this composer.

Giacomo Carissimi, *maestro* at the Church of St Apollinare in Rome, was at the same time the most serious and the most successful of seventeenth century oratorio writers. The appreciation of humane values was at all times a pressing concern of post-Renaissance art. In the expression of such values a high critical acumen is called for. This Carissimi would seem to have possessed. The flavour of his music is of imaginative academicism, for there is the freshness which came from observation of and judicious selection from the experiments of others and the maturity of older habits. Carissimi, whose conservatism led him to drape a mass round the superannuated stolidity of *L'Homme Armé*, balanced the shape of oratorio by elevating the chorus to a position of dignity comparable to that of the solo voice. Apart from the historic significance of this gesture there was the aesthetic gain in that the deft sculpting of recitative and aria is thrown into deeper relief and, potentially, there were psychological implications. But for their realization we have to wait for Handel. Carissimi in small space, in *Daniele*, *Jephthe*, and *Jonas* for instance, achieved briefly impressive representation of mob instinct and impulse. Elsewhere, in the detached commentaries of *Jephthe*, he provokes the other, critical function of choral interpolation. If it is necessary to moralize in so special a form as oratorio then the chorus, impersonal, is the proper agent. The adventurousness of Carissimi is exemplified, in a dialogue between Democritus and Heraclitus, by a momentary patch of bitonality. Coloratura is controlled by rhythmic organization on the one hand and by an attentiveness to verbal significance on the other. Above all one notices the absorption of instrumental accentuation into choral and vocal style. It is in these respects, and especially in rhythmic pointing, that the last part of the seventeenth century contrasts most violently with the earlier period. By the last quarter of the century one realizes that the free *melismata* of pure lyricism are restrained by the regular pulsation of the dance. The foundations of classical music are, in fact, laid.

We must not fail to understand that technique at all points was subordinated to the factor of audience gratification. With an untutored and prejudiced public this entails either lowered standards or disillusionment for the composer, but in general and despite fairly frequent lapses, the audiences concerned with the music detailed in this book were knowledgeable and also practically educated. The music of Carissimi will now fall on deaf ears. Then it was different. Della Valle attended the church of St Apollinare on Christmas Eve, 1640;

though by arriving late he was obliged to stand the whole time in a very great crowd, he remained there with the utmost pleasure, to hear the excellent music that was performed. In the beginning he was particularly enchanted by the *Venite exultimus* [sic], which was more exquisite than words can describe. 'I know not', says Valle, 'who was the author of it, but suppose it to have been the production of the Maestro di Capella of that church' [i.e. Carissimi].

The capacity for stirring emotional depths, possessed by Carissimi, may briefly be expressed in the opening of the departing recitative of Jephtha's daughter.

2.

Plo - ra - te, plo - ra - te col - les, do - lé - te, do -

- le - te mon - tes et in af - flic - ti - o - ne cor - dis me - i

u - lu - la - te

This work, and probably others by the same composer, came to the approving notice of Handel. So also did those of Alessandro Stradella, whose *S. Giovanni Battista* was an essay of considerable importance. But Stradella's gifts as a composer—his style was near that of Carissimi, with an inclination to ground bass, fugato, and *da capo* planning in aria, but of wider range—have preserved his fame less effectively than have his amorous proclivities his notoriety. Stradella, having successfully filched the affection of a Venetian nobleman's *inamorata*—no mean feat—was driven to sanctuary (with his Hortensia) in Rome. The injured lover, left in Venice, endeavoured to re-establish at any rate his dignity by hiring a pair of assassins to liquidate the errant Stradella. They proceeded to Rome and, their intelligence being sound, to the church of St John Lateran. There they arrived to hear a performance conducted by their intended victim. The performance was probably of the above-mentioned oratorio. This was too much for villainy, even in seventeenth century Italy; their hearts softened and their daggers dropped from inert fingers. 'An instance', remarks Burney, 'of the *miraculous powers* of *modern* music, superior, perhaps, to any that could be well authenticated of the *ancient*.' These adventures, handed down in the loose folds of the gossip of three centuries, were eventually memorialized in two dead operas and a still more dead novel.

It is said that Stradella was a favourite composer of Purcell. However that may be, he was acknowledged by Handel, who borrowed from his ideas. The general circumstances which created the environment in which Handel was to find himself have been stated. It remains to discuss the influence of the greatest of his predecessors.

Chapter Two

HANDEL IN ITALY

TO be an Ottoboni was to hold such a place in society as can (or perhaps, could) only be occupied by scions of noble and ancient families well exercised in the arts of graft, nepotism, and self-interested diplomacy. Three Ottobonis were, one after the other, raised to the Chancellorship of the Republic of Venice (the family was of Venetian origin). The last of the Chancellors had a son, Peter, whose elevation in 1689 to the papacy set the family name on the most supreme roll of honour. Cadet members of the clan were beneficiaries in more than honour.

Alexander VIII no sooner was upon the Throne, than he instantly sent for all his relations, and afterwards enriched them. *Don Antonio* was declared General of the Forces of the *Holy See;* his Brother *Don Marco*, General of the Gallies, and Duke of *Fiano*. *Peter Ottoboni, Don Antonio's* son, and Grand Nephew to the Pope, who had lived with him as a private Gentleman in St *Mark's* Palace, was called to the *Vatican*, where the Pope ordered him a magnificent Apartment. At first, he appeared abroad only [!] as a Prelate for some Days, but the Pope afterwards created him, not only a Cardinal, but Superintendent General of all Affairs in the Ecclesiastical State, and Legat of *Avignon*. He gave him likewise the Post of Chancellor of the Holy Church, though *Innocent* XI had abolished this Employment, for the Good of the Apostolical Chamber. This Post is for life, and, besides other Perquisites which may be made, brings in a Revenue of 14, or 15,000 *Roman* Crowns a Year. This Cardinal likewise, during the sixteen Months of his Uncle's Pontificate, received of the Rents of four Abbeys,

with so many other Ecclesiastical Benefices and Pensions, as makes his
Revenue actually amount to 80,000 Crowns a Year.

At this moment Ottoboni is a hero without a plot, but
de Bainville's enthusiastic pen brings the Cardinal nearer to
our theme.

He has the natural Quality of all *Venetians*, that is, he is a good
Politician. He has an exquisite Sense of Humour, and loves to appear
and to make himself valued. He is liberal, obliging, well-behaved to
every body, and very affable to Strangers, whom he receives in the
most complaisant Manner at his House. He loves Poetry, Music, and
Men of learning; so that every Fortnight he holds, in the Palace of the
Chancery where he lodges, an Academy of learned Men, at which
several Prelates and other learned Persons generally assist. . . . His
Eminence likewise keeps in his Pay, the best Musicians and Performers in *Rome*, and amongst others the famous *Archangelo Corelli*, and
young *Paolucci*, who is reckoned the finest Voice in *Europe;* so that
every *Wednesday* he has an excellent Concert in his Palace, and we
assisted there this very Day. We were served with iced and other
delicate Liquors; . . . . But the greatest Inconveniency in all
these Concerts and Visits, is that one is pestered with swarms of
trifling little *Abbés,* who come thither on purpose to fill their Bellies
with those Liquors, and to carry off the Crystal Bottles, with the
Napkins into the Bargain.

In the scramble for iced drinks de Bainville might have
rubbed against the broad shoulders of George Frideric
Handel, but his manner of writing left little scope for
digression from the principals in courtly society. We are,
while lamenting the lost opportunities of historical portraiture (too little is known of the youthful Handel, after
all, of far more significance than the Cardinal), driven back
to the hard road of scanty fact. Handel was in Rome in 1707
and frequently to be seen at Ottoboni's receptions. He was
twenty-two years of age and had been resident in Italy for
a year. The reason for an Italian visit should be apparent
from the contents of the preceding chapter. Italy was the
European post-graduate school for composers. And already
Handel had shown himself adept in the Italian manner.

Handel arrived in Italy with a *Laudate pueri* (in F) which
he had composed long ago at Halle. This little work, the

oldest music extant in Handel's autograph, is a school piece after the manner of a Scarlatti cantata for solo voice but, despite much mechanical manipulation of commonplace roulades and consecutive thirds, quite exquisite on the ear. One moment, where German humility, awe, and wonderment produce passages of interrogatory rumination to the text 'Quis sicut Dominus, Deus noster, qui in altis habitat et humilia respicit in coelo et in terra?' shows a maturity beyond the average of apprenticeship. An exalted theme of jubilation may be compared with the later treatment of the same word in *Messiah*. In youth Handel rejoiced thus:

which may be used by the vocalist reader as a touchstone for his or her potentialities in coloratura.

At this early period of his life Handel contrived to come into contact with many who were influential. On account of acquaintance with Gastone dei Medici he was able to present his credentials to Gastone's more prosperous brother Ferdinand, Grand Duke of Tuscany. At Florence, a musician lived under the shadow of Alessandro Scarlatti, who had recently been court composer—though his more recent operas had not commended themselves to the Grand

Duke. The studious Handel, who rarely let slip an opportunity of increasing his technical knowledge, must have
eagerly scanned the scores of such an acknowledged master.
The *Laudate pueri* had been modelled on the Scarlatti style and
was re-written in 1707 after closer acquaintance had revealed
more of the suave and masterful idiom of the master.

Scarlatti refined and defined the aria; he obliterated the
gaucheries of antique melody; he carried music drama from
the limited ranges of awkward realism to the condition in
which music is allowed to speak for itself in terms of music;
he, as well as Corelli, enlarged the technique of stringed
instruments by using them in the manner suggested by vocal
music; one stage further, he allowed onomatopoeics to
suggest novelty in orchestration.

Handel contracted Scarlattina, passed through all the
obvious phases while in Italy, and never lost traces of the
infection.

Two Handelian works which must have caught the
Roman ear were the *Dixit Dominus* (dated 11 April 1707) and
the revised *Laudate pueri* (8 July 1707). In these, and
particularly in the first, there is the unmistakable imprint.
The opening of *Dixit Dominus*, gravely resplendent with
arpeggio figuration placed in G minor, has the characteristic
motif of regality. Albeit here God the King is also God
the Judge and the introduction strikes a minatory note
suggestive of the German theological background to
Handel's religious philosophy. A further touch of German
solemnity comes with the binding chorale motive which runs:

4.

do - nec po - nam in - i - mi - cos tu - os

sca - bel - lum pe - dum tu - o - rum.

Handel used this canto fermo device generously in later oratorio. Had Handel lived permanently in Italy he would have become an Italian composer as in England he became an English composer with, of course, an evident strain of cosmopolitanism. There is one remarkable harmonic sequence in the *Dixit Dominus*, Mozartian rather than Handelian, subtle and almost painfully sweet.

With this may be compared the Catholic devotion of the *Salve regina*, another work of the same period. Here perhaps is the most eminent display of pure religious emotion in the whole range of Handel. The clergy endeavoured to prose-lytize Handel. He protested eternal devotion to the church of his fathers but it is clear that he possessed a strong respect for the sad beauty as well as the glad exhilaration of the Catholic faith. Here is his act of devotion to the 'Glorious virgine, of alle floures flour'.

6

It was Rome which called from Handel his greatest
Italian compositions and it may be suspected that Roman
society with its charm, culture, and hospitality appreciated
the capacity of Handel for understanding the Roman point
of view. He was the ideal composer because he could
adapt his style to the requirements of the community
with which he was concerned. What there is of his
German music is Germanic; his Italian music Italian;
his English music English; and (if reports may be
trusted) his Irish music Irish. This sense of locality
(local colour is, perhaps, too strong) was one secret of
Handel's success.

Early in 1708 Handel was in Rome enjoying the

hospitality of Pietro Ottoboni and the Marquis (or Prince) di Ruspoli, the collaboration of Cardinal Panfili and the respect of the Arcadians. Progress in the esteem of the cardinalate was probably engineered by an earlier friend of Handel—the famous priest-musician Steffani, who, as a professional diplomat and a notable ecclesiastical administrator was likely to furnish a good reference for any of his friends and protégés in Rome. The Arcadians received the fruits of Handel's contact with Panfili, which took place under Ottoboni's roof, in the May of 1708. The work, described as an oratorio but in truth a morality in masque form, was *Il trionfo del tempo e del disinganno*. The reactionary text hardly stimulated Handel and the resultant work is scarcely comparable with others of the same period. Fifty years later Handel revised it and added several numbers of great individual interest. But, even so, *Il trionfo* or *The Triumph of Time and Truth* may be written off as a relative failure. The Arcadians were polite but not enthusiastic. They had loved *La resurrezione*. *Il trionfo* was an anticlimax and, in any case, everybody was anxious to get out of Rome in the early summer of 1708. Yet another investment of the city was imminent.

La resurrezione, Italianate but not subserviently Italian, had been given at the home of the Prince di Ruspoli—the Bonelli Palace—a month before *Il trionfo*. In this little work we see the beginnings of the Handelian oratorio proper and we detect the approach of the composer to the philosophic problems with which he was to deal in greater detail later in life. Music, we learn, and especially dramatic music, is for Handel a representation of life. Behind the sinuous pleasantries of this essay stands a strong humane interest, an implicit intention to reveal to man the nature of man. Characteristically a fallen angel is metamorphosed into a complete and intelligible human being, while Lucifer's sparring partner, the angel proper, carries charm and

ebullience in music which possesses no obvious supernatural interest.

The constitution of religious music is beyond the power
of criticism to define. For the greater part of his life Handel
was content to set out for inspection the nature of man.
Sometimes he shows the divinity in man, which would
appear to be no mean exercise in spiritual apperception; at
other times he unwraps the Satanic element, but, because he
proceeds from the premise that man has in him the real
duality, he is one of those rare creatures 'that will use the
devil himself with courtesy'. The advantage of Handel's
peculiar and personal technique in psychological analysis
lies in the fact that we start from the familiar, from ourselves,
and discover the ramifications of our own thought in
picturesque symbolism. For most men the attributes of
God are inaccessible save through parable. The genius of
Handel, and also the attractiveness of Handel, depends on
the fact that his mind rarely moves outside the ambit of the
common. But his imagination isolates the salient and enshrines it in permanency.

The style of Handel is, doubtless, Baroque but his
sense of humour and his native thoughtfulness allow
him frequently to linger over detail with Gothic concentration. It is with the mind of a medieval that Handel looks
at Lucifer: the technique of caricature which turns
Lucifer into a gargoyle, with very human face, is a
transmutation of medieval practice. And this is a devil of
attractive lineament.

That diabolism is not self-evident in the music may, of
course, be ascribed to immaturity rather than to an un-
willingness to meddle with the unseen and the intangible,
yet, here and there, a dramatic flash shatters the conventions.
Lucifer's opening 'Caddi ver' has nothing remarkable other
than its range. The succeeding recitative, however, brings
an early example of Handel's economical understanding of
picturesque brass interpolation.

squar - cia le ten - de   al - la tar - tar - ea not - te

The same recitative takes us remotely to Stygian darkness *via* the unexpected route of C sharp minor. The obviousness of the method is helpful to the imagination and it may be noted that while Handel was frequently at pains to make himself clear, his auditors have of late years refused his guidance and have dragged external irrelevancies across the trail and thus have found many wrong turnings. *La resurrezione* is religious not because it deals with a biblical theme but because, in the real world, it arouses sympathy, together with an awareness of the hidden beauty of the unseen world. The wide-eyed wonder of the medieval marginal commentator is immanent. The angel who admonishes Lucifer enjoys a virtuoso triumph in 'Disseratevi o porte' which steps outside the limits of theological argument and thus exhibits delicious femininity.

8.

Angelo (Sop)

Ce - de - te   hor - ri - de

Ob Solo
Violini
unisoni

Bass

The graciousness of this idiom leads to a commonly unappreciated facet of Handel's character—his gentle courtesy, his chivalry. The appearance of Mary Magdalene is not only effective because 'Notte funesta' succeeds Lucifer's 'O voi dell'Erebo potenza orribili' which, with swishing glissandi in the strings temporarily lets hell loose, but also because the scene dramatically changes in the orchestration. Deprived of the complete paraphernalia of opera, the intrinsic quality of the music in oratorio must be superior to that which in opera is partially relieved of explanatory function by the versatility of the scene painter. Hence the importance of orchestration. Hence the two flutes and gamba which attend the entrance of Mary Magdalene. The charming berceuse character of the aria 'Ferma l'ali' (muted strings are added to the previous scoring and the cembalo is held in reserve until the half-way mark is reached) rides over a long tonic pedal and enshrines a delicacy of thought moving in its simplicity. The mourning women are exhorted by St John in terms of much less musical interest. St John has an unfortunate and undeniable tendency to exhibitionism—as much the fault of the singer as of Handel, no doubt—and his superfluous semiquavers have the flavour of ineptitude. In passing, however, the cello counters the voice with a pleasant obbligato in 'Quando e part', while 'Non frangendo va per l'onde' has the scenic sense of the title contoured in the melody.

It must be confessed that, from time to time, in the course of this work, interest flags. Probably only because we see it in wrong perspective. The dialogues in recitative, for example, become tedious and this tedium suggests a practical and artistic reason for the later reliance on choral interpolation to break the monotony of later oratorios. Not that choruses are entirely absent from *La resurrezione*. There are two. And it is difficult to decide which is the worse. Both are conventionally operatic in that they say nothing which can be accepted as within the terms of reference. Somnolent clerics may quite well have been roused from inadvertent slumber by such music as comprises the concluding chorus.

Here it is not the cheerfulness that is at fault but the perfunctoriness.

La resurrezione is an early work and an unequal work, but this is not to suggest that it should remain in oblivion. Its friendliness is sympathetic and its directness an antidote to aesthetic introspection. The lambent grace of Mary Magdalene, the naïve horrifics of Lucifer, the angelic aspirations, the delight in variety of orchestral pigmentation and the buoyancy of melodic invention show the healthy ebullience of a youth of twenty-two. And there is more to it than this. There is the earnest of belief in the certainty of the universal significance of Easter Day.

The Italian music of Handel is final in its Italian-ness. It is contained within a chapter of Handel's life. Something of the style is carried forward but the difference between the music written in Italy and that written in England is the difference between the Church of Rome and the Church of England, a difference in gravitation. Handel in Italy is in the line

Carissimi, Palestrina, Clari, Pergolesi . . . and more of the same school. The old choirs of Italy re-open upon us, and pour forth their peals and appeals to heaven, in all their grandeur, and softness, and affectionate entreaty; now splendid as the other pomp of their service, now flowing as their robes, now tender, and breathing away in aspiration, as the perfume in their censers.

Thus Charles Lamb expressed his appreciation of the great tradition in reviewing the *Fitzwilliam Music* (see *New Monthly Magazine*, Vol. xvi, p. 327).

Chapter Three

ESTHER

THE progress from ambition to achievement depends in some degree on fortunate accidents of acquaintanceship. Handel had a large capacity for friendship and he was frequently under obligation to his friends. As a young man—when first he came to England he was twenty-five— he cultivated, as many do, the influential but this was only one side of his personal relationships. He possessed the invaluable faculty of allowing his imagination to be fertilized by other men's ideas.

During the reigns of Queen Anne and the early Hanoverians ideas were common currency in England. It was possible to live on them. Ideas were acquired at the University, at the Inns of Court, at the theatre, at the *bagnio* (opportunities for gaining experience were surprisingly generous); the tyro tested his early stock in the school of the wits or in the pages of the *Spectator* or the *Gentleman's Magazine*; later there were publishers, Tonson or Curll or, if you were a musician, Walsh, who would purchase the first fruits of individuality, plagiarism or imagination. In general there was a tradition in the mutual exchange of worth-while knowledge. The intellectual aristocracy of wits, poets, philosophers, musicians, and statesmen thrived on this intellectual free trade—only possible because no veneration for specialization had arisen to atrophy the

43

concept of a gentleman as a man of many parts. This was because learning was sufficiently compact for the intelligent person to go into it fairly deeply at various points, and to keep abreast of current ideas while drinking coffee or chocolate at White's or Button's in the morning, and port at home or abroad in the evening. It should be made clear that we are dealing with a privileged section of eighteenth century society: there was a less encouraging side to the picture. Nevertheless, the period was one in which sociability was respected.

Handel came to England fresh from Italy and it is worth while seeing the position through his eyes. Italy was a land of violent contrasts, of wealth and poverty, of intelligence and ignorance, of scepticism and credulity. The outlook was in the broad sense of the word, conservative. England was politically the most progressive and civilized country in Europe: it was also the commercial centre of Europe. Thus the difference which would have been noted was more than a geographical difference. If we may analogize there was as much contrast between the two countries as at present there is between a recently liberated nation, inspired by new and fierce ideals, and a neutral state which has retained something older and mellower from the pre-war years. The measure of Handel's English citizenship is his gradual absorption of English ideas. Unconsciously maybe, but unmistakably, his oratorios become individual in form and expression because they reflect the feelings, emotions, and ideals of his contemporaries.

It is only part of the truth to ascribe Handel's supremacy in the English music of his time to high technical brilliance; of great importance is the fact that he was, as we should say, a good mixer. And here we may momentarily appear to be in conflict with the conventional portrait of the man. That he was on occasion brusque, if not actually rude, is possibly true (biography as a rule magnifies the exceptional in such cases as that of Handel in order to support the premise that genius is either mannerless or mad—or both), but it is

difficult to believe that in an age when spades were unam-
biguously named, even in the presence of ladies, he was
thereby either remarkable or censorable. An Augustan
gentleman, after all, was one who could choose the occasion
for misbehaviour. The circle of Pope, Arbuthnot, Swift, and
Gay, to which Handel had early access, was a debating
society in which points of order with regard to etiquette
were not raised. From intimacy with this literary fraternity
grew the pattern of English oratorio.

We must for a time continue on a literary basis. For
English music is perversely rooted to literary ideals and
therein lies its independence (for the most part) of the main
European stream and to this may be attributed its lack of
favour in foreign parts. The English madrigal differs from
the Italian, as does the pre-Handelian anthem from the
Italian motet, in an almost syllabic interpretation of text.
Nor is this merely a matter of accentuation and allusive
picturesqueness. It inclines to a deeper philosophical level,
prompted by the acceptance of the educated of the supremacy of the written word to other forms of artistic
expression. Byrd surely endorses this unuttered opinion
when he writes (and incidentally he was by no means
incompetent in literary expression) 'there is a certain hidden
power, as I have learned from experience, in the thoughts
underlying the words themselves; so that, as one meditates
upon the sacred words and constantly and seriously considers them, the right notes, in some inexplicable manner,
suggest themselves quite spontaneously'. Again Byrd
recommends that good vocal music should be 'framed to the
life of the words'. This literary approach, despite such
august patronage, is no guarantee of great music, but it is
indicative of an attitude which is vitally different from the
fundamentally abstract and purely musical premises which
supply the impulse to classical writing. Byrd and Handel
(and for that matter Purcell, Elgar, and Vaughan Williams)
are great musicians whichever way they may be approached,

D

but it is at least helpful to take into account their extra-territorial interests.

By 1720 Handel had had ten years experience of English life and his acquaintance with English literature was sufficient to allow him an appreciation of the works of John Gray (he was a subscriber to *Poems on Several Occasions*, which appeared in that year), a poet of some importance to Handel in more ways than one. His feeling for the tradition of English music had found practical outlet. There were the *Birthday Ode for Queen Anne* (1713)—a tribute as much to Purcell as to the queen, the *Utrecht Te Deum* (1713) and the magnificent dozen of Chandos anthems (1716-18).

This occasional music impressed on Handel two facts. First, that ceremony of State, unsurpassable in dignity, was a part of the English way of thinking and that ceremonial music was a contributory factor to such elegant advertisement; second, that the English Bible was similarly a national heritage and the basis of a great deal that was noble on the one hand if moralistic on the other. Appreciation of the situation made Handel an Erastian and a bible student. For some years after his arrival there was opera to be considered. As elsewhere, and since the lamented death of Purcell, this was after the Italian manner. Handel came with the original intention of providing operas for the English market (until 1742 he did this with varying degrees of success) but as his sojourn lengthened from a respite from Hanoverian dullness into protracted residence and thence to naturalization it became apparent that the native amalgam of pride, prejudice, and patriotism (not solely the political variety) was likely to make the way of the opera composer difficult. Handel was sufficiently English to achieve acceptable equations in compromise. On the left hand side of the equation opera *minus* movement, *plus* vernacular text: on the right hand side—oratorio. Before this was presented to the public, private exhibitions were demonstrating congenial conclusions.

In the summer of 1720 *Acis and Galatea* and *Haman and Mordecai* (later to be known as *Esther*) were performed in the tree-girt seclusion of the Cannons estate. The former, by no stretch of imagination, can be considered as oratorio (although not infrequently it is sung in accordance with the fallacious principles which inspire many singers of oratorio), and was labelled, with aptness, a Serenata in one place, a Pastoral in another, a Pastoral Opera in a third, and finally a 'Mask'. Thus there is ample choice in classification without falling into the trap of the zealous who mistake (an implication from style in performance) *Acis and Galatea* for a work about God. One more point of objection. If there is one work of Handel's which suffers more from re-orchestration than another it is this. The light and ephemeral score of the original is naturally infectious with the gay and improvisatory brilliance of the age and the man.

The chief interest for us in this work is the method in which Handel, for the first time, tackles a non-official, lyrical and imaginative libretto. Despite its courtly manner, Gay's theme touches more than the metamorphosed naturalism of the *salon:* it looks ahead to Keats in effluence of coloured detail. A Devonian, perhaps, could hardly fail to glance beyond the conventions of pasteboard boscage.

When Polyphemus addresses Galatea we enjoy three lines of imperial dignity—out of Nahum Tate—and five of gracious accuracy in naturalistic observation:

> *Thee*, Polyphemus, *great as* Jove,
> *Calls to Empire and to Love,*
> *To his Palace in the Rock,*
> *To his Dairy, to his Flock,*
> *To the Grape of purple Hue,*
> *To the Plumb of Glossy Blue,*
> *Wildings which expecting stand,*
> *Proud to be gathered by thy Hand.*

Handel, with his known affection for rural scenery and his

amateur interest in its pictorial representation, must have found refreshment in such verse and contrast to the aridity of many opera libretti.

Contact with the Earl of Burlington's literary lions must have been a stimulating experience. The valuable part of history and biography is that part which remains unrecorded and what Pope said to Gay and what Handel said to the two of them on musico-literary matters rest in the repository of ungarnered *obiter dicta*. But there are gambits in conversation which may be deduced. The essays of Steele and Addison, the excursion of the latter into the field of musical criticism and libretto invention (once Handel had looked at Clayton's score of the ill-fated *Rosamund* he could explain its failure in brief, emphatic castigation), the pamphlets of Swift and Arbuthnot, the new Shakespearian criticism of Dennis, the Spenserian editing of John Hughes—an acquaintance of Handel at Thomas Britton's musical evenings—and the numerous translations which brought Racine and Corneille within the experience of those theatre-goers whose education had stopped short at the acquisition of the French language. Colley Cibber, Edward Smith, Ambrose Philips, and a host of obscurer lights had translated, and produced, with some freedom, various French dramas during the years of Handel's English pupillage. Therefore that Pope (or Samuel Humphreys) should try his hand at Racine's *Esther* was not surprising. Nor, perhaps, was it surprising that Handel should see therein a subject for music. (There is only a thread of documentary evidence that Pope was the author and the bad craftsmanship would seem to contradict it.) What Pope thought, if we accept his authorship, may be conjectured from his notable distaste for music in general, yet he apparently placed no difficulties in Handel's way.

Haman and Mordecai was written and composed and eventually performed at Cannons. A detail of incidental interest is that this subject was once the basis of a religious music drama by Hans Sachs. So Colley Cibber informs us and in so doing reminds us that our story begins far back in history.

Esther (for the final title must be adopted now in the interests of convenience) calls for detailed comment as the parent of all English oratorios. Now the paradox of Handelian oratorio is this. Common categorization details it as religious whereas the aesthetician protests that this classification is untruthful, oratorio being opera under camouflage. The correct conclusion is that the two points of view are not incompatible, although their protagonists frequently are.

It may appear that Handel had an aptitude for serving both God and mammon. If he did, it was because experience had taught him to believe that human nature was reflective, in many of its facets, of the divine. His contribution to philosophy centred upon the apotheosis of humanity. It is a Romantic habit (and we should place Handel on the side of the Romantics if compelled to discuss him in Classical-Romantic terminology) to proceed from the *terminus* man with the ultimate intention of deducing a deity. Handel had this progress frequently in mind, but he had also a preconception of his deity. His maternal grandfather had been a Lutheran pastor; therefore he grew up to a sternly judicial concept. The pietism of his university (theology at Halle was vigorously taught and discussed) urged the intimacy of the personality of God; Italy His glorious attributes. In England one moved either among agnostics or optimists; the latter believing in a complacent version of British Israelitism—the English being the specially favoured race. The free range of thought leads many to the consideration of such varied visions. To possess permanently one vision requires either especial grace or especial stupidity. Handel was neither exceptionally endowed with grace nor with stupidity. He was thoughtful, charitable, and frequently assailed with doubt. His music is expressive of these characteristics and much of it is centred round the problems of divine relationship by the very fact that his oratorios were rooted in the Bible (he was a particular reader of the Bible—as on one occasion he reminded the Archbishops of Canterbury and York), and also that he was accustomed to the assimilation of the ideas which underlie verbal expression.

Esther is a perplexing work. It may be assumed that others found it so in view of its relegation to the list of impracticability. It possesses little of the recreational content of the formalized opera; it carries the deportment of the anthem, particularly of the rich Chandos type, into realms of hysteria; it puzzles with orchestration both subtle and eclectic. It is a romantic essay framed in an unromantic period. It may be assumed that in 1720 it would have been regarded, by all but a minority of the highly imaginative, as outrageous in modernity.

The greatness of Handel often reposes in monumental untidiness. His robust nature overlooked the assertion of posterity that orderliness was a *sine qua non* in the (miscalled) Augustan era. Thus the termination of *Esther* is in an elephantine chorus as proportionate to the oratorio as a whole as is the overgrown south transept of Chester cathedral to the parent body. And yet, implies Handel, if deliverance from persecution provokes an act of thanksgiving then let the demonstration be generously endowed. By the side of 'The Lord our enemy has slain' the 'Hallelujah' chorus looks small. Incidentally there is a family likeness between these two movements in that both lie in D major (the proper key for eighteenth century jubilation), both hammer at eternity with quaver repetition, and both stretch out long lines of canto fermo to correlate the interstitial flourishes.

Memory would hold this finale because it is of the quality generally accepted as Handelian. The greatness of the movement, however, is but one side of Handel and that not the

most important. Sensitivity recollects the startlingly imaginative preluding of Esther's first appearance on the stage
(if we may assume that the first performance was enacted).
In this, it may be suggested, lies more clearly the
characteristic Handel.

After a lengthy passage of cheerful piety (the Jews being
ignorant of Haman's machinations), which includes a 'Praise
the Lord' of pleasantly direct laudation complete with harp
accompaniment, Esther is announced indirectly. The
dramatic technique is here adroit in its suggestion that we
are already acquainted with our heroine. In the revised
version of 1732, however, we are introduced immediately
to Esther through exhortation to the gales and rills, then to
silence, to peace—the peace which resides in Esther's soul.
The murmurous incantation of flutes, oboes and bassoons,
echoed by strings and harp,

reminds one of the rare enchantment of a summer landscape
left by a glimpse through the plain diamonds of an un-
coloured window in a village church: the entry of the voice
brings in slender contrast the virginal simplicity of

11.

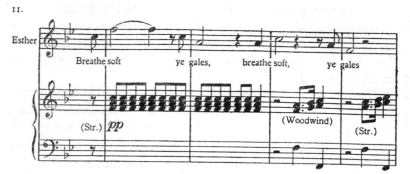

Esther

Breathe soft   ye gales,   breathe soft,   ye gales

(Str.) *pp*   (Woodwind)   (Str.)

The more metaphysical association of ideas which succeeds brings a touch of impressionism not far in spirit from the idealism of Debussy.

We are at once in love with Esther and the dramatist-musician has achieved his first aim. Consistency of characterization is an attribute of the later Handel (although in 1720 he was hardly immature) and Esther fails to maintain her initial delicacy.

The central pages of the score (from here we consider the more ample revised version) are magnificent in conception and execution. Esther arrives at a moment of tension. Haman has, as the Priest puts it, sent forth his decree. The sons of Israel all shall in one ruin fall. The chorus moves from the role of protagonist to that of observer and in a brief episode, which leaves an illusion of length on account of its suspension over a 12/8 adagio rhythm, turns to strains of woe and foreboding. Esther ruminates on the situation in a melancholy air, enhanced at the natural climax by a solo flute and by the tearful accent of dragging violin chords. Then she pleads with Ahasuerus. The duet 'Who calls my parting soul from death' rides over an insistent bass which again is illusory, this time of a ground. Like many parts of the oratorio this duet is borrowed from the *Passion* of 1716, where it occurs as a duet between Mary and Jesus. It happens that this music comes at impressive moments in both works, as does a subsequent air by Haman. At this stage it should not be necessary to emphasize the fact that no music is *per se* sacred. Our guide to this virtue is always the associations of propriety. The progress of the music from 'Breathe soft, ye gales' through a darkening key sequence brings the duet with Ahasuerus into correct focus, reminding that items in oratorio and opera should not in general be separated from their context, and we marvel at the certainty which thickens so dramatically the chordal texture, makes sombre the rhythmic pulse, weighs down the scale of emotion with unprecedented chromatics and edges the whole atmosphere of poignancy with an exquisite thrust of sorrow from an Italian sixth.

12.

At this point we should retrace our steps to catch the threads of the plot. Haman, the Agagite, was high in the favour of the king Ahasuerus. He hated Mordecai, guardian

and kinsman of Esther. He resolved to exterminate the Jews
on account of a private spite against Mordecai and, so easily
was responsibility delegated even in those days, that
accordingly he issued a decree 'to destroy, to slay, and to
cause to perish, all Jews, both young and old, little children
and women . . . and to take the spoil of them for a prey . . .
and the king and Haman sat down to drink; but the city of
Shushan was perplexed'.

The sequence of events is not unfamiliar, nor was it
entirely unfamiliar to Handel who, as a boy, had heard of
the discrimination against the Jews by Louis XIV. He had,
as future oratorios will show, more than a merely artistic
sympathy towards this people and a strong humanitarianism may legitimately be felt to underlie the presentation of
the plot. That the overture was regarded as an integral part
of the drama is demonstrated by the exposition in the first
movement of the rhythmic formula which accommodates
Haman's initial utterance. The second movement, if sequel
is looked for, may in rather general terms be regarded as
premonitory of the doleful 'O Jordan, Jordan, sacred tide';
the association appears but faintly on paper but in performance, with the intermission of varied music, the return of
G minor in broad, melancholic effusion is sufficient to recall
the mood of the overture. Chrysander places the significance
of the three movements of the overture thus: (1) the wickedness of Haman (2) the complaints of Israel (3) deliverance.
The arrogance of Haman is epitomized in his first statement.

13.

Let Jew-ish blood   dye ev-'ry hand,   Let Jew-ish blood

dye ev-'ry hand,   Nor-age,   nor sex   I spare

Having launched the drama he retires, witnesses the development of the conflict from the wings and is produced again for the third act. Here a suppliant, he petitions Esther abjectly and with chromatic extravagance. The music is that which in the *Passion* is given to Jesus in the garden of Gethsemane. The differences between the two versions are instructive. The jagged ♪♪♪♪♪ rhythm of the *Passion* gives way in *Esther* to the inexorable tread of level quavers. Handel had reason for such alteration but it is only to be found beneath the surface of the music. In the *Passion* the manhood of Christ, the reality of the Agony, the acuteness of the pain to the seeing believers are all drawn in the nervous tension of the uneven rhythm. Haman's case is one which admits of no doubt, nor at this moment, of sympathy. He has been tried and convicted in his absence; his fate is inevitable; his plea for clemency is both dramatically and historically necessary but that it is of no avail the grim equality of the pulsation clearly indicates.

Handel, however, rarely dismisses his villains without a look, at least, of sympathy and in the dignity of 'How art thou fall'n' Haman passes to the gallows bearing the admiration of those who can wonder respectfully at the bravery of the wicked. Sometimes Handel wonders with Edmund whether 'we were villains on necessity, fools by heavenly compulsion, knaves, thieves, and treachers by spherical predominance . . .'

There are other points to reveal dramatic mastery. Esther's spirited reply to Haman—a study in varied stresses and rhythmic emphasis; her gentle prayer in the sweet aria—'Watchful angels' where the arpeggio-shaped melody, poised over a 39-bar pedal and supported by a translucent accompaniment of strings *senza cembalo*, *theorbo e harpa*, makes the words almost superfluous; there is, also, a theatrical Hallelujah, written originally in Italy, which is of surpassing brilliance.

It is beside the point to labour that *Esther* is an opera in all but name. Handel's achievement lies in his interpretation of the conflict which lies behind the conventions of the libretto prepared for him. What he appears to revivify is the biblical narrative. To read the Authorized Version and to compare its poetry with that of Handel is to discover that both belong to the same world. The barbarism, the splendour, the intrigue, the rough justice were beyond the powers of any eighteenth century dramatist, but not beyond those of Handel. It may be said that this first oratorio is religious in that it is faithful to the significance of the Book of Esther: it is not religious in that it expresses no moral exhortation. It is factual as unbiased history, it is warmed by the human interest of precise portraiture. But such conclusions as are to be drawn we must draw for ourselves.

There are some externals which may be considered. First the ascription to Pope. The sole evidence for this is an advertisement in the *Daily Journal*, 19 April 1732, which, repeating an advertisement for the first public performance of *Esther* of two days earlier, adds 'the words by Mr Pope'. The word-book of the 1732 performance informs us 'The additional words by Mr Humphreys', while another tradition brings into this field of uncertain authorship the name of Dr Arbuthnot. Beyond stating that the text would seem to have come from a committee of friendly writers we can only let the matter rest in dubiety until such time as additional evidence is forthcoming. Also a matter of uncertainty is the date of the Cannons performance. The *Weekly Journal* for 3 September 1720 refers to the opening of the Duke of Chandos's chapel 'with an Anthem on Monday last (August 29)'. It is an open question whether *Esther* can be considered as an anthem: after all a gossip writer can hardly be expected to be academically precise. But divine service in addition to *Esther* sounds a longer operation than would have been acceptable even in those leisurely days.

There is one more interesting point. *Esther* contains a harp part.

This may be considered as the first 'modern' work (harps formed part of the medieval orchestra and survived until Jacobean days in broken consort) with a harp in the score. It indicates, particularly if we bear in mind the scoring of *Giulio Cesare*, a point of view which would have gained the appreciation of Berlioz. Further there was the harpist. He was a Welshman, Powel by name, and one of a family of virtuosi on this instrument. He was respected by Handel who, in addition to using him orchestrally, wrote for him a concerto (published as an organ concerto—Op. 4 no. 6). Clearly Powel was at Cannons about the year 1720, when the set of suites was published which include the so-called 'Harmonious Blacksmith' variations. Now the legendary blacksmith was also named Powel(l). For various excellent reasons the familiar story is discredited, but one is loth to dismiss a tradition outright. Facts suffer distortion if entrusted to memory, but something of the truth remains.

In this case there seems reason to believe that Handel was inspired by a man called Powell to the composition of certain music and the 'Harmonious Blacksmith' variations may come into this category. Of further interest is the remarkable similarity between 'Happy we' from *Acis and Galatea* and the Welsh folk-song 'Codiad yr haul'.

In the year of Handel's death we discover a young student endeavouring to keep abreast of modern music by studying —or at least purchasing—what was nearly forty years old. James ('Parson') Woodforde noted in his accounts for the year 1759 the following assortment of items:

```
May 25 A New Wigg      £1  1  0
June 16 Had of my father  £1  1  0
June 18 Nosegays      £0  0  1
July 4 Ester Oratorio   £0  5  0
July 5 Messiah      £0  5  0
July 6 Two White Waistcoats  £1  16  0
```

The sandwiching of oratorios between nosegays and waist-coats brings up an important observation. Handel was accepted domestically (he was the most popular of eighteenth century composers according to publishers' lists) as were his contemporary novelists. And it was this fact as much as any other which produced the Handelian complex of later music lovers.

Chapter Four

DEBORAH AND ATHALIAH

IN the twenties and thirties of the eighteenth century English society underwent, partly through similar political circumstances, the same febrile course as we endured at the corresponding period of the twentieth century. The auspices were against any probability of oratorio capturing popular imagination. *Esther* was heard, heard of, and forgotten. But time has its revenge. The counter-attractions to Handel's music were led by Heidegger who, with plain intent to capitalize vice, offered easy opportunity to the willing to part with money and virtue at balls, at ridotti, at the opera house, and in places of less repute. Leisure for these occupations was afforded by the rule of Walpole, who contrived to give to a not particularly grateful people the blessings of peace. In so far as he was a public entertainer Handel drew benefit from this state of affairs and it should be remembered that he was no puritan, but a friend of Heidegger. On the other hand he was unable to refrain from looking at purely musical problems. So we discover in the operas, and particularly in *Giulio Cesare* and *Riccardo I*, notable excursions in orchestration, some of which are also apparent in the score of *Esther*.

But the future of opera was made uncertain by the furore of *The Beggar's Opera* in 1728. This effusion of Gay pricked the bubble of absurdity which topped the unintelligible

59

narratives of alien poetasters and stimulated the growing
discontent at the imperious and expensive reign of alien
singers. More than this, *The Beggar's Opera* humanized the
dramatic-musical alliance. It may be said that, whereas the
stiff, decorative formality of opera pictured that odd blend
of art and emotion typical of the baroque, the licentious,
devil-may-care *sans culotterie* of the ballad opera revealed the
ranging imagination that was to urge human affairs into the
Romantic classification. Handel, with his multifarious
contacts, recognized that there was something to be said, in
England, in favour of departure from a never very popular
tradition. Addison had expressed as long ago as 1707 what
was frequent matter for complaint for twenty years.

> *Long has a Race of Heroes fill'd the stage,*
> *That rant by Note, and through the Gamut rage;*
> *In Songs and Airs express their martial fire,*
> *Combate in Trills, and in a Feuge expire;*
> *While lull'd by Sound, and undisturbed by Wit,*
> *Calm and serene you indolently sit;*
> *And from the dull Fatigue of Thinking free,*
> *Hear the facetious Fiddles Repartie:*
> *Our Home-spun Authors must forsake the Field,*
> *And Shakespeare to the soft Scarlatti yield.*

There is no reason to suppose that Handel dissented from
this feeling, for while he was trained as an operatic composer, he found little incentive in that field to develop his
own personality. Or, in the interests of strict accuracy, we
should say that deviation from the easy tunefulness of the
Bononcini work, or the Scarlatti *pasticcio* was not favoured
by the complacent audiences who attended Vanbrugh's new
theatre in the Haymarket because it was a convenient place
for meeting friends and acquaintances. One could talk
through opera performed in a language which one could not
understand, provided that the music was not too loud
(Handel's, they said, always was too loud): but *The Beggar's
Opera* being both funny and intelligible as an attack on

Walpole's government encouraged attention. The direct tunefulness of familiar ballad strains was also pleasant for its own sake in contrast to the elaborate divisions of Italian melody. But for Handel ballad opera was a little too near nature for him to adopt. Although he patronized it and was reported to have shown vigorous symptoms of enjoyment, he was an artist. Serious opera in the English language was an alternative idea but hitherto this prospect had limped through a zealous attachment to the machinery of the Italian method. Addison himself had blundered into the inconsequences of *Rosamund* (1710); Hughes, another acquaintance of Handel from the Britton circle, had created the pedantry of *Calypso and Telemachus* (1712) and damned its chances with the tag *An Essay for the Improvement of Theatrical Musick in the* English *Language, after the Model of the Italians*; in 1727 Lewis Theobald, victim of the most romantic couplet in the *Dunciad*, showed more initiative in blending opera and pantomime within the limits of *The Rape of Proserpine;* and in 1732 Henry Carey wrote, with Lampe as musical coadjutor, *Amelia*—'a sort of adaptation of Beaumont and Fletcher's romantic tragi-comedy to the realm of opera'. It was within the limits of this form of expansion that *Acis and Galatea* was pirated by Thomas Arne's father in 1732. If opera was unsuccessful there was a chance that opera plus ballet (Handel tried this before he retired for good from operatic composition), opera plus pantomime, opera plus the pastoralism of Ovid, or some other variation would catch public interest on the rebound from the limits of boredom. But the groundwork of any new musical art form must be operatic.

In the small London of 1728 hardly any artistic event or publication could escape notice. To realize this it is only necessary to contemplate the activities of a modern community of comparable size—with less than half a million inhabitants. In the year in question John Ernest Galliard (whose name is more promising than his music), a

E

Hanoverian who anticipated the immigration of George I by fifteen years, produced an oratorio based on Milton—the *Morning Hymn of Adam and Eve*. One may assume that Handel noted the gesture within the confines of his absorbent memory. Of this work Burney remarks, 'I must say, that I never saw more correctness or less originality in any author that I have examined, of the present century, Dr Pepusch always excepted'. The publication of Galliard's work was succeeded by a setting of the same text by 'a grave and decent man, remarkable for his affability and gentlemanly deportment', a notable conservative following Purcell and Blow rather than the refinements of Italian example—an organist named Philip Hart. But once again no one, unless the composer, thought this a notable contribution to musical literature.

However, two swallows are more suggestive of summer than one and two quasi-operatic works attached to poetry with religious bias were provocative of experiment along similar lines. And so we meet Bernard Gates, master of the children of the Chapel Royal, a devout Handelian possessed of a score of *Esther* and a nice taste in honorifics. Handel's birthday, in 1732, was celebrated privately at Gates's house in James Street, Westminster, with a representation—*with action*—of *Esther*. The chorus, drawn from the choirs of the Chapel Royal and Westminster Abbey, 'was placed after the manner of the ancients, between the stage and orchestra; and the instrumental parts were chiefly performed by Gentlemen who were members of the Philarmonic [*sic*] Society. After this, it was performed by the same singers at the Crown and Anchor, which is said to have first suggested to Handel the idea of bringing Oratorios on the stage. And in 1732, *Esther* was performed at the Haymarket, Ten Nights.'

The names of the choirboys who assisted at these historic functions deserve memorial, not only on their own account but also on that of the generations of their compeers who have fed the tradition of English music. Three of them gained honourable mention in adulthood: John Randall, who became Professor of Music at Cambridge; John Beard, whose attachment to Handel was lifelong; and Samuel Howard who grew up strong in the faith that English music was the best in the world and 'never listened to foreign artists or their productions'. James Butler, John Brown, Price Clevely, James Allen, Thomas Barrow, and Robert Denham, however, vanished into the obscurity which cages the reputations of all those who fail to come within the environs either of fame or notoriety. The Dean of the Chapel Royal apparently proscribed oratorio with action, for his jurisdiction over choirboys put him in this position of authority. But one should credit him—he was also Bishop of London —with tolerance for allowing the boys into the ill-famed atmosphere of the Haymarket. Bishop Gibson, with his *ipse dixit*, pointed the manner in which the Handelian oratorio should develop.

One wonders whether Bishop Gibson had heard of the complaints of Mme de Maintenon that representations of Racine's *Esther*, with music by Moreau, had disordered the propriety of her religious house. One also wonders whether Handel had come across the score of Moreau's music. Certainly the fact that Moreau's music for both *Esther* and *Athalie* was highly respected and frequently performed in France raises fascinating possibilities.

It was on 5 December 1732, that Aaron Hill, an exact contemporary of J. S. Bach and a poet, playwright, scholar, as well as a particular admirer of Handel, wrote to the latter as follows:

Sir,

I ought sooner, to have returned you my hearty thanks, for the silver ticket [of admittance to the opera], which has carried the obligation farther, than to myself; for my daughters, both such lovers of musick, that it is hard to say, which of them is most capable of being charm'd by the compositions of Mr *Handel*.

Having this occasion of troubling you with a letter, I cannot forbear to tell you the earnestness of my wishes, that, as you have already made such steps towards it, already, you would let us owe to your inimitable genius [already commemorated by Hill in the Ode to Handel of February 1, 1732], the establishment of *musick*, upon a foundation of good poetry; where the excellence of the *sound* should be no longer dishonour'd, by the poorness of the *sense* it is chain'd to.

My meaning is, that you would be resolute enough, to deliver us from our *Italian bondage;* and demonstrate, that *English* is soft enough for Opera, when compos'd by poets, who know how to distinguish the *sweetness* of our tongue, from the strength of it, where the last is less necessary.

I am of opinion, that male and female voices may be found in this kingdom, capable of everything that is requisite [Hill was among the Senesino baiters]; and, I am sure, a species of dramatic Opera might be invented, that, by recruiting reason and dignity, with musick and fine machinery, would charm the *ear*, and hold the *heart*, together.

Such an improvement must, at once, be lasting, and profitable, to a very great degree, and would, infallibly, attract a universal regard, and encouragement.

I am so much a stranger to the nature of your present engagements, that, if what I have said, should not happen to be so practicable, as I conceive it, you will have the goodness to impute it only to the zeal, with which I wish you at the head of a design, as solid, and imperishable, as your musick and memory.

This, no doubt, was the opinion of many, more qualified to discuss music than Hill. He, however, had occasion to communicate to Handel and could not refrain from passing such suggestions on.

There was clearly no lack of incentive to produce at least one successor to *Esther*. Samuel Humphreys has already introduced himself in relation to the additions to *Esther* and during the 1732 opera season he translated the text of *Rinaldo*. Humphreys had an enthusiasm for translation greater than his skill (his translated *Peruvian Tales* (1734) were symptomatic of the distant tread of Romanticism), an appreciation of Prior, which led to a life of that poet (1733), and a capacity for flattery. He had put out *Verses on Canons* in 1728—this gives a clue to an acquaintance with Handel of long standing—and gained thereby the approval of the susceptible Chandos. Handel is said to have 'had a due

The Oratorio of Judith by Defesch (1732)—from an engraving by Hogarth

esteem for the harmony of his numbers'; but this probably means that Handel found in him a collaborator without too much spirit. Handel felt it strongly when certain librettists regarded this or that oratorio as their particular project. On 17 March 1733 *Deborah*, text by Humphreys, music by Handel, was put on at the Haymarket. The *Daily Journal* of April 2, which mentioned the visit of the royal family, detailed the work as an opera. It is worth pointing out that Deborah as an historic character had been enshrined a few months previously in the music of Maurice Greene, an individual misunderstood and mistrusted by Handel. There is no reason why Greene's subject should not have stimulated the fancy of Handel.

In point of interest *Deborah* should rank lower than *Esther*. The plot is less immediately appealing. One mad woman—Deborah; one treacherous woman—Jael; one puppet soldier—Barak; a more independent fighter and a more interesting character—Sisera, who, unfortunately worshipped the wrong god, and one old man—Abinoam, are the principal *dramatis personae*. The Book of Judges makes terrifying the battle between Israelites and Baalites and the original song of Deborah and Barak is as wild, and as outstretching, as anything by Blake. Humphrey's rhymed couplets can be as pedantic as:

> *By that adorable decree,*
> *That chaos cloth'd with symmetry;*
> *By that resistless power that made*
> *Refulgent brightness start from shade*
> *But still'd contending atoms' strife,*
> *And spake Creation into life;*
> *O thou supreme, transcendent Lord,*
> *Thy succour to our cries afford.*

That, part of Deborah's first invocation, is hardly remarkable unless it be for the prevision of the fifth line. Nor can the following extract, Jael's recapitulation of her homicidal technique, lay claim to dramatic power:

*Then was I conscious, Heav'n, that happy hour
Had placed the foe of Judah in my pow'r:
The workman's hammer and a nail I seiz'd,
And while his limbs in deep repose he eas'd,
I through his bursting temples forc'd the wound
And rivetted the tyrant to the ground.*

Humphreys was ahead of his time in dullness and this may have contributed something to the lack of appreciation which met *Deborah*. But the 'bald and barbarous language of the old vulgar version' would have lost its 'venerable sacredness' in the theatre. Paradoxically, therefore, the Handelians were forced by literary and religious sentiment to the acceptance of an 'improving' technique detrimental to the dramatic expression for which they pined.

The first moment of musical interest comes with the overture: that is if one is prepared to associate the principle of leitmotive with Handel. The second section re-appears as an Israelite chorus and the fourth as one for the followers of Baal. Too much should not be made of this fact. Probably the intention had a dramatic basis, but there is always the chance that Handel found time pressing, inspiration flagging, and a couple of useful ideas lying about. *Deborah* is, in fact, a convenient example of Handel's capacity for serving up Sunday's joint in Tuesday's fricassee. Three choruses ('The great King of Kings', 'O celebrate His sacred name' and the 'Allelujah') belong originally to the Coronation Anthem 'The King shall rejoice'—perhaps a subtle interpreter would see herein an intended compliment to George II. The *Passion* supplied a proportion of the solos—it would have been a pity to waste the good music which had been tied to Brockes's libretto. So far as *Deborah* is concerned, the adaptation of old material is comfortable and indeed, supposing the listener to be (a) possessed of a retentive memory and (b) perspicacity, emphasis is given to particular points of emotion. For instance, the homily on sin, delivered by the Daughter of Zion (*Passion* no. 50) suits

Deborah admirably for her reply to Sisera (*Deborah* no. 30).
An interesting readjustment brings a pointed and climactic
use of a 6/4 at the end of the first phrase,

14.

Haugh — ty ty - rants are but dust;

while the final phrase of the same song provokes apposite
discord:

15.

Place   in   van - i - ty____ their trust.

Bach used discord as a necessary ancillary to musical
logic, Handel as a factor in dramatic statement. Therefore Handel, using as stage apparatus what to another
composer is essentially musical, is relatively economical with
his discords. None the less he is masterly and methodical
in handling the problems of dissonance.

The close relationship between opera and oratorio is
particularly evident in *Deborah*. There is a general super-
ficiality about the solos which would matter little in stage
performance where characters take bodily shape and appropriate uniform. Removed from most of the helpful
properties of the stage the images blur into uncertainty.

Barak borrows the conventions of the familiar stage hero
and struts into battle proclaiming 'All danger disdaining, for
battle I glow' to a manly formula of convenient martial
proportions. Unfortunately the manliness is, to us, somewhat impaired by devotion to another convention. Barak
and Sisera are contralto parts. Deborah herself is an obvious
prima donna. She is adorned with bejewelled irrelevancies,
one of which—the exquisite 'Choirs of angels' (another loan
from the Daughter of Zion of the *Passion*)—with its sophis-
tication and voluptuousness makes it difficult for us to
visualize the barbaric prophetess. Abinoam, in contrast to
the other characters, is dramatically alive—the prototype of
a long line of senatorial impressions. Old men (they were all
basses) became a feature of oratorio and Handel treated them
alike with grave respect and gentle sympathy, betokening
a natural courtesy. Paternal pride rings in the spacious vaults
of 'Awake the ardour of thy breast'. In 'Swift inundation
of desolation' an angry fist is shaken at the enemies of
Judah while at the other extreme of emotion Abinoam
weeps in affecting gratitude (to the unusual accompaniment
of *organi*) through the simple beauty of 'Tears such as
tender fathers shed'.

So far as his chorus was concerned Handel employed a
relatively small number of singers and he treated them with
flexibility. It was a unique occasion when the choristers
of the joined cathedral choirs took part in the Dublin
Messiah. As will be seen from the list of their names (see
p. 128) they numbered fewer than forty. The broad contrasts
between massive choral effects and interspersed exhibitions
of virtuosity (or incompetence) by solo singers is a fancy of
a later time than that of Handel himself and ignores the
possible nuances contingent on treatment of the body of
performers as a unified corps under one command. Handel's
chorus needed to be elastic in outlook and dramatically
intelligent, for it fulfilled a variety of functions. It personated
the Children of Israel or the Priests of Baal as the occasion

warranted; it adopted the neutrality (with the neutral's right
of moral observation) enjoyed in Greek drama by the chorus,
in Shakespeare by the fool, or in Bach (and in the Handel
of the *Passions*) by a somewhat detached Christian believer.
In *Deborah*, because we are as yet hardly emancipated from
the operatic chorus, the choristers are continually participant
in the action and the eight part writing is intended not as an
addition to musical weight but as a token of the numbers
pressing into the crowd scenes.

It is seldom that Handel falls back on quotation from
chorale (the notable exception is the Funeral Anthem for
Queen Caroline), or other traditional melody, but he frequently contrives to give an analogous impression of public
utterance by the introduction of bold fragments of melodic
elementalism. Such fragments occur in *Messiah*—'The Lord
gave the word' and the 'For the Lord God omnipotent
reigneth'; *Israel in Egypt*—'I will sing unto the Lord' and
Samson—'Let their celestial concerts all unite', and in
Deborah in the opening chorus. Later on, in 'Plead thy just
cause', we light, fortuitously, on a simplified enunciation
of the opening of 'O come, O come Emmanuel'.

16.   c.f. ex. 4, p. 33.

Plead   thy   just   cause____   thy   aw - ful   pow'r dis - close

It is in the employment of such apparent commonplaces
that we see the beginning of Handel's universality. The case,
incidentally, is the same with Beethoven. But it is not the
artlessness which effects durability: it is the art. In short the
melodic material attracts the general listener and the initial
directness and economy commands his attention during the
subsequent working-out. The native habit of assessing
Handel by his choruses is probably not an unfair way of
arriving at an estimate of his genius. But as well as the
inspired simplicity there is the subtlety which turns
simplicity into complexity.

'Immortal Lord of earth and skies' succeeds the overture.
The key change in itself is elevating—from B flat to D
major. The presentation of majesty, either earthly or divine,
calls from Handel a consistent pattern of prelude. Hence we
recognize a permutation on the first figure of 'Zadok the
Priest'. It is a convenience to recognize the suggestive
function of such phrases, because the strong pictorial element in eighteenth century music in general, and in Handel
in particular, depends on their ready acceptance. Handel is
as studious in definition as Wagner, but less loquacious. In
the melancholy comment of the priests of Baal on the ill
success of their cause we find that particular broken rhythm
which details dejection, the chromatics significant of emotional tension, the diminished seventh of death (no composer can use this familiar emblem of crisis with more
discretion or point), the doleful vacillation of the Neapolitan sixth,

17.

and symbolic silences. The gravity of the accompanying
organ should also be noticed.
   The choruses of *Deborah* are of varying interest: some are

mere stock models (1733) from the Handel factory. But
there are some of magnificent originality. When, for
example, the Israelites prepare for the arrival of Sisera in
'Despair all around them' they choose, in realization of the
first word, the 3/4 rhythm of uncertainty, and hint at the
illustration of dubiety by syncopation—a feature of the
chorus in *Saul* which describes that king's decline into madness. The opening chorus of Part II is one of those massive
diptychs. The first section describes Sisera: the second calls
for action. The fugal finale, both musically and dramatically
inevitable, is joined to the first part by the rhythmic tautness
of

18.

Ja -cob a -rise, Ja - cob a - rise, as - sert thy God, And

scorn op-pres-sion's ı ron rod,

Effectiveness in performance depends on resilience
in the hortatory iterations of 'Arise' and on insistence
on the dramatic concatenation of consonantal vigour in
'And scorn oppression's iron rod'. An antique (or Scottish)
i-ron in place of the politely emasculated *i'on* makes the
difference between artistic life and death. In passing, one
may mention the regal arpeggios attached to Sisera in the

first part of this great chorus, but this time they are grimly set in the minor.

As an ensemble the valedictory 'All your boast will end in woe' is remarkable. Not on account of its musical content so much as for its dramatic organization. This quartet *cum* chorus takes up music where opera left off and demonstrates possibilities of climax which find complete realization in *Jephtha*.

Deborah was a popular subject in the years 1732-3. In addition to Greene's setting and Handel's oratorio there was a farce—*Deborah or a Wife for You All*—put on at Drury Lane on April 6.

The more one studies successive works by Handel the more one is brought to a realization of the certainty of his intentions. An understanding of *Messiah*, the work with which most of us unfortunately start our appreciation of the composer, can only reach completeness if regarded in relation to the rest of his works in the same genre, just as the ninth symphony of Beethoven must be seen in the light of the previous eight. From *Deborah* to *Messiah* is a considerable step, but the approach by way of *Athaliah* widens our knowledge considerably and offers certain facets of style which, wrapped in the texture of the major works, illuminate the imagination. There is a definitiveness in the overture to *Messiah*, more subtle than that contrived by the leitmotive mechanism, which is clear only under the conviction that Handel's overtures were more than curtain-raisers.

Deborah is significant in this connection. So, too, is *Athaliah*. The difference between the two is that the former is obviously picturesque whereas the latter is suggestive by implication. The first movement is a slashing allegro and no harm is done if the tempo is meteoric. An overture comprising two allegro movements is improper according to the tenets of the French and Italian schools, but Handel was never remarkable for subservience to custom and the overture in question (it has no fugal section—to complete the tally of omission) only fits *Athaliah* because it is formed as it is. The glitter, the barbarism which surround the story are there, for *Athaliah* is pagan and oriental.

Humphreys again attempted to provide a textual base for Handel's operations but his is an egregious performance. The chasm between him and Racine (from whom the plot is taken) is both deep and wide. *Athalie*, first performed at the Théatre Français in 1716, had been translated into English in 1724 by William Duncombe (this translation was reprinted in 1726 and later in 1746).

Handel's second study of Racine indicates his attentiveness to general intellectual habits, for the stage was under strong Francophile influence—in marked contrast to political affairs. Moreover we have a guide as to Handel's approach: it was not that of the pious Bible reader, but that of the general student of art and literature.

The glory of *Athaliah* lies in its characterization. *Athaliah* herself is a type, later reproduced in Storge and Dejanira, particularly congenial to Handel's pen. A woman of (may this be deduced from the robustness of the music?) magnificent physique, of singularity in determination, of violence in commingled anger and jealousy, and impregnate with superstition. Athaliah parallels, femininely, Saul and, in similar manner, catches sympathy. Racine (Act II Scene V) leaves us in no doubt on this point of sympathy.

> *Sur d'éclatants succès ma puissance établie*
> *A fait jusqu'aux deux mers respecter Athalie;*
> *Par moi Jérusalem goûte un calme profond;*
> *Le Jourdain ne voit plus l'Arabe vagabond*
> *Ni l'altier Philistin, par d'éternels ravages,*
> *Comme au temps de vos rois, désoler ses rivages;*
> *Le Syrien me traite et de reine et de soeur;*
> *Enfin de ma maison le perfide oppresseur,*
> *Qui devoit jusqu'à moi pousser sa barbarie,*
> *Jéhu, le fier Jéhu, tremble dans Samarie;*
> *De toutes parts pressé par un puissant voisin,*
> *Que j'ai su soulever contre cet assassin,*
> *Il me laisse en ces lieux souveraine maîtresse.*

This queenly speech, and any suggestion of its content, is omitted by Humphreys who prefers to simplify the issue to an unrelieved tale of treachery. This process, which has its attractions in libretto construction—assuming considerable powers on the part of the actor—is comparable to that by which a film script derives from literary sources. There being no action possible in oratorio, Handel was left with the task of putting back, in musical terminology, what of Racine had been left out. In Athaliah's first appearance it can be seen how completely he does it. After her dream interview with Jezebel, Handel refers back, in an accompanied recitative of great puissance, to the possible reserves of strength and power. Dismay, self-pity, but also majesty emerge from

19.

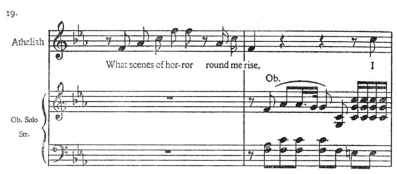

that frees the wretch from woe, to Maj-es-ty a-lone a foe?

This is music apt not only for Athaliah but also for
Calphurnia: it is in fact of universal application. The scene
(Scene III) which introduces Athaliah is one of Handel's
most penetrating psychological studies, to be compared
with those other terrifying studies of mental disturbances
in *Orlando* and *Saul*. The interspersed choruses of Attendants
and Sidonian priests are ingratiatingly beautiful and in
character sycophantic. Thus they are contributory to
Athaliah's state of mind. These choruses, as are most of the
oratorio choruses, are plainly operatic—though impossible,
and the point needs frequent emphasis, under the operatic
conventions of the period. The peculiar aptness of idiom
to emotion is most adequately represented, perhaps, in the
lush opening of

20.

Athaliah is oblivious of this encouragement to optimism.
She is haunted by the dream vision of the living Joash, he—
the king elect of Judah—whom she had imagined dead.
Mathan, the apostate priest, continues to console his dejected
queen. 'Gentle airs, melodious strains' calls exotically for
accompaniment of solo cello (an accepted symbol of
melancholia), archlute, bass, and cembalo. Athaliah recalls
herself from reverie and answers Mathan in the aching
protestation of

Soft - est sounds ... no more can ease me

Then Mathan proposes action. To the Temple, he cries, to destroy the usurping infant, and the Attendants rally round with stirring battle cry:

The trai-tor if you there des-cry, The trai-tor if you there des-cry,

To which, as so often happens in Handel's illustration of Baalite-Israelite strife, the Allelujah inspired by Joash in the succeeding scene makes unconvincing reply. To be quite fair,

F

however, the remaining Israelite choruses are magnificent, instinct with the prodigious power of those in *Israel in Egypt* and co-ordinated with athletic orchestral accompaniment. 'The mighty power in whom we trust' (with a thirty bar introduction ripe for a concerto grosso), 'The clouded scene begins to clear', 'Around let acclamations ring', and 'Give glory to his awful name' are Handelian thunderbolts. The Germanic choralism (with chorale hints) of

23.

Let ev - 'ry voice His praise pro - claim

set against an ornate Italian background was to give way in the later works to a less antithetical relationship between choir and orchestra, but the early simplicity, culminating in the Funeral Anthem, is tremendously moving.

It will be remembered that *Athaliah* was first performed in Oxford on Tuesday, 10 July 1734. The invitation to visit Oxford came to Handel from the Vice-Chancellor—Dr Holmes. It is suggested that this was a gesture to display a Hanoverian attachment normally alien to a university in which Jacobitism had its most fervent adherents. *Athaliah* with its literary and dramatic interest would appear to have been a happy choice of subject for the occasion. Whether or not the oratorio was designed especially for Oxford, it is impossible to discover. One can only put forward the possibility that this might have been the case. *Messiah*, after all, was apparently composed particularly with the Dublin performance in mind. Further we may draw attention to the date of the completion of *Athaliah*—7 June 1734. If Handel had been invited to write a work for performance in the Sheldonian and if the political background had been brought to his notice as assuredly it would have been, the propaganda value of 'Around let acclamations ring' seems high, as may be appreciated from this excerpt:

Deborah and Athaliah 79

The singers were Cecilia Young (she married Arne in 1736)
as Athaliah, Strada as Josabeth, Carestini as Joad, the boy
Goodwill as Joash and Waltz (the cook) as Abner. If his
cooking was as efficient as his singing must have been, to
encompass the terrific impulses of 'When storms the proud',
Handel's table must have been well appointed.

It is customary to look askance at such a work as *Athaliah*
(*Susanna* is in similar case) and to regard it as a misshapen
opera. But the nearer it approaches to the fundamental
emotional expressiveness of operatic technique, the more it
appears to fulfil Handel's intention: opera in English was
the objective set before him by his friends. Oratorio form
was the ultimate point of achievement possible within the
social, literary, religious, and theatrical terms of reference
within which he worked.

The denouement of *Athaliah* is a masterpiece of musical
climax. The attempted kidnapping of Joash and the conse-
quent defeat and death of Athaliah are difficult of comprehension from the dreary text of Humphreys; the music,
however, is self-explanatory.

From 'Around let acclamations ring' we proceed to the exultation (couched ominously in a rough-edged C minor) of Abner, to the poignant simplicity of Mathan's realization of the failure of his deity—the modulation to B minor cuts coldly across Athaliah's last hope to the cataclysmic death song of Mathan—which should be compared with Jephtha's 'Open thy marble jaws'—and finally to Athaliah's brief death agony.

Athaliah herself supplies the major musical interest of the work, but nowhere—and here the contrast with *Esther* is marked—are there signs of weakening control over the architecture. The work is a unified whole. But round the main plot are ancillary themes and picturesque ideas. There is the chorus of virgins whose charms clearly hit the eye through the ear and there is the fondness—without biblical sanction — between Josabeth and Joad. They deal apparently with the main purpose of the story but actually with private and personal affairs. If one of these duets may be selected especially it is 'Softest joys'. This is, strictly speaking, an irrelevance, but history is humanized by its presence. A high priest who could pontificate with such effect; and his wife, with her skill in preserving the rightful king of Judah from destruction, had surely earned their right to connubial bliss.

It was at about this time that Hogarth rudely cartooned an oratorio team other than Handel's. Imitation is one form of flattery. In 1733 Defesch had produced *Judith*. Actually he was a better fiddler than composer; he led the band in 1745 for the *Occasional Oratorio*. After the unfortunate Defesch, came Porpora with his *David*. 'Some of the choruses and recitatives', says Mrs Pendarves, 'are extremely fine and touching, but they say it is not equal to Mr Handel's oratorio of *Esther* or *Deborah*.' In 1735 these works, with *Athaliah*, formed the repertoire for the first regular season of oratorio. *Esther* was given six times, *Athaliah* five, *Deborah* three. The theatre was Covent Garden which Handel had

*Handel directing an oratorio rehearsal
from the harpsichord*

taken for his operas in the earlier part of the year when a cabal of opinionated nobles had wrested the Haymarket from him. To ensure full houses, Handel made the innovation of playing organ concertos between the acts of his oratorios.

Chapter Five

SAUL AND ISRAEL IN EGYPT

The greatness of Lear is not in corporal dimension, but in intellectual: the explosions of his passion are terrible as a volcano; they are storms turning up and disclosing to the bottom that sea, his mind, with all its vast riches. It is his mind which is laid bare. This case of flesh and blood seems too insignificant to be thought on; even as he himself neglects it. On the stage we see nothing but corporal infirmities and weakness, the impotence of rage. While we read it, we see not Lear, but we are Lear: we are in his mind, we are sustained by a grandeur which baffles the malice of daughters and storms. In the aberrations of his reason, we discover a mighty irregular power of reasoning, immethodized from the ordinary purposes of life, but exerting its powers, as 'the wind bloweth where it listeth', at will upon the corruptions and abuses of mankind.

THUS Charles Lamb exhibits the panorama of intellectual imagery which lies behind all great, humanistic, and tragic art and if we choose to invite him to present a background to Handel's *Saul* it is because he was a Handelian on the one hand and a critic on the other, whose generous vision transcended the artificial barriers which departmentalize the arts. It is precisely the lack of this broad vision which has reduced Handel to the proportions of an inflated sacred cantatist. The tragedy of Lear is, *mutatis mutandis*, the tragedy of Saul: the greatness of Shakespeare a yardstick by which may be measured the greatness of Handel.

To recognize the sublimity of *Saul* it is necessary to refer to the intellectual and not the corporal dimension of the subject. The study is not of Saul alone but of the devastation of human happiness by cankerous envy. The vision is Aeschylean in that the moral issues are wrapped in action and in personification; Shakespearian in that the personification is alive and cast in terms of familiarity. The drama rides on two levels—the human and the divine or, if you will, the human and the superhuman.

It is tempting to link the emergence of *Saul* and its companion work *Israel in Egypt* with Handel's catastrophic illness of 1737. For in 1738 Handel appears to have changed from extraversion to introspection. The opera writer, conscious of the seen pattern of life, changes into the oratorio composer (there were still two operas to come, but the form was out of favour), the analyst of disembodied motives and aspirations. Herein will be detected the particular virtue of the oratorio method. The illusion of tangible reality is removed by the exclusion of the actor's mimetic talent, but not so far removed as to be inaccessible. Handel discovered compensation in the variety of natural musical movement for the lost stimulus of physical movement: he also disclosed that drama may lie within music alone, and more subtly, rather than in the admixture of music and conventionalized drama. This conclusion may be drawn from comparing the one Handel with the other—the operas with the oratorios. The former are episodic: the latter unities. It is fascinating to bribe sensuousness into acceptance of Handel the oratorio writer by staging, as operas, his oratorios, but aesthetically it is inadmissible.

The intellectual emphasis (for we may proceed phrase by phrase with Lamb) in *Saul* is determined in large part by the extra-territorial influence of the chorus. In the two greatest choruses the singers are without the drama, impartial and disinterested judges. 'Envy, eldest born of Hell' is surely the most directly fearsome movement in the whole of Handel. The inexorable tread of the ground, the isolation of the crucial words—envy, hell, hence (the librettist's assonance is a powerful aid to concentrated emphasis), the turgidity of the middle section, the anger of the gesturing wraith in the violin *glissandi* merge into an immensity of observation that is terrifying. The technique has been familiarized from previous Handel: the genius lies not in novelty but in co-ordination. There is nothing here that is obvious: at the same time there is nothing that is not obvious. The Envy chorus supervenes at the point which displays the scheming of Saul to destroy David (it is a little difficult to be other than surprised at the extreme self-righteousness of Handel's most unsoldierly conception of his hero): it opens the second part of the oratorio and has the effect of summarizing, by implication, the preceding plot.

The next chorus of major importance—'O fatal consequence of rage'—is placed equally dramatically. After David has pleaded the excuse of a festival in Bethlehem to avoid an interview with Saul, the king, his fury worked higher by the partisanship of Jonathan, attempts the death of his own son. Then the chorus, watching destiny like fateful Norns, strike with the tonal ambiguity of

25.

f   O   fa - tal   con - sequence of   rage

describe in brief physical dimension the monstrous proportion of their subject (herein we recall the monster Polypheme, from *Acis and Galatea*) and wander into the nomadic and Brahmsian conclusion—first cousin to the middle section of the *Song of Destiny*. This clairvoyant music seems to catch something of Bishop Berkeley's philosophy: and here it may be mentioned that Berkeley, born in the same year as Handel, had come to England for the first time in 1713—at which point in history Handel also was learning to find his feet in English society—had associated with Swift and Pope, and had published his *Theory of Vision* in 1734.

The explosions of Saul's passion, if less volcanic than those of Lear, are none the less terrible. Through the course of his moral decline runs the power of inevitability, implying that his descent is not entirely due to faults of his own but equally to the malignancy of fate or circumstance. 'With rage I shall burst' pictures the surface anger which most of us find difficulty in suppressing. And in the Saul of 'A serpent in my bosom warmed' we see ourselves, finding Saul therefore a likeable character, until, anger overleaping all its normal bounds, the final cadence is furiously unleashed.

This aria is deliberately and symbolically unbalanced: the man is presented, for the first time, as possessed of unreason. The next appearance of the king underlines the theme of growing madness by emphasis on cunning. We hear the magnificent deliberation of the false oath 'As great Jehovah lives'. Skilfully Handel maintains our interest in his principal character by using him with discretion. His actions, his motives, his thoughts are dealt with for the most part indirectly—except for passages of recitative—until the solemn and awful moment arrives when Saul is converted to belief in the possible efficacy of witchcraft. Here is the climax.

> *Wretched that I am! Of my own ruin author!*
> *Where are my old supports? The valiant youth*
> *Whose very name was terror to my foes,*
> *My rage has drove away. Of God forsaken*
> *In vain I ask his Counsel! He vouchsafes*
> *No answer to the sons of disobedience!*
> *Ev'n my own courage fails me!—Can it be?*
> *Is Saul become a coward?—I'll not believe it:*

And then—

Across the years Handel looks at Marlowe and Saul at Dr Faustus—

> *. . . The stars move still, time runs, the clock will strike,*
> *The Devil will come, and Faustus must be damn'd.*
> *O, I'll leap up to my God! Who pulls me down?*
> *See, see where Christ's blood streams in the firmament!*
> *One drop would save my soul—half a drop: ah my Christ!*
> *Yet will I call on him: O spare me, Lucifer!*
> *Where is it now? 'Tis gone; and see where God*
> *Stretcheth out his arm, and bends his ireful brows!*
> *Mountains and hills, come, come and fall on me . . .*

The devils came to Faustus: Saul goes to the Witch of
Endor.

The drama of the emotional climax is obvious in abstrac-
tion in Handel as in Marlowe: each example within its
context, and within the conventions of the eighteenth or the
sixteenth century, is inspiring—the more inspiring on
account of the technical restraint. Greatness has no need to
step out of simplicity to express profundity.

In a valedictory publication Sir Henry Wood emphasized
the functional artistry of recitative. The dialogue between
Saul and the Witch is illustrative of this.

28.

The shaping of the melodic fragments is pertinent, picturesque, and cumulative, while the sombre approach of the ghostly Samuel is famous for its forwardness in orchestration. Three bassoons are employed. The Dead March, again the orchestration is potent, needs no words to describe the universality of its immediate simplicity. Saul has gone, as he came, with dignity—trumpets and trombones cast a mantle of glory round his spirit: *de mortuis nihil nisi bonum.* The honour paid to death, implies Handel, is token of the brotherhood of man. So is death swallowed up in victory.

The difficulty of *Saul* is that Saul himself is peerless in stature. Our sympathy is with him—it is a frequent practice of Handel to enlist our sympathy for the unfortunate—and against David and Jonathan, neither of whom are assisted by the pallor of their lines and the relative lack of distinction in their music. Merab (Handel appreciated young

women with independent minds) is the only minor character to emerge from the music with a defined personality.
The conclusiveness of 'My soul rejects the thought with
scorn'—Merab's haughty and defiant rejection of her
father's proposal of marriage with David—recalls Esther's
treatment, musically and mentally, of Sisera.

The first three scenes of *Saul* represent one of Handel's
most extensive pictures. The canvas is crowded with life.
The overture, either an organ or an oboe concerto in fact,
preludes the C major approach to pageantry. C major is the
key of the Epinicion on the one hand, of the Funeral March
on the other. And midway between the two the Battle
Symphony also echoes this key. Whether by accident or
design the strategic positioning of this key aids unity. We
have here the somewhat rare consistency of beginning and
ending an oratorio within the same tonal limits.

Saul, a large subject, uses a large orchestra, including
three trombones, carillon, kettle drums borrowed from the
Tower of London, and with a separate organ part. It was
often urged against Handel, as against almost every great
master of orchestration, that he was noisy. Charles Jennens,
who arranged the libretto of *Saul*, wrote feelingly on his
personal experiences as Handel's host at a time when Handel
was particularly concerned with developments in instrumental colour.

Mr Handel's head is more full of maggots than ever. I found yester-
day in his room a very queer instrument which he calls carillon
(Anglice, a bell) and says some call it a Tubalcain. I suppose because
it is both in the make and tone like a set of Hammers striking upon
anvils. 'Tis played upon with keys like a Harpsichord and with this
Cyclopean instrument he designs to make poor Saul mad.

This and the next item, combined with Handel's lofty
treatment of Jennens as poet, nearly made poor Jennens
mad as well as Saul. The letter continues:

His second maggot is an organ of £500 price which (because he is
overstocked with money) he has bespoke of one Moss of Barnet. This
organ, he says, is so constructed that as he sits at it he has a better

command of his performers than he used to have, and he is highly delighted to think with what exactness his Oratorio will be performed by the help of this organ; so that for the future instead of beating time at his oratorios, he is to sit at the organ all the time with his back to the Audience.

Jennens, writing thus with an air of assumed superiority to his kinsman the Earl of Guernsey, reveals more than he intended. There is Handel experimenting, in Wagnerian fashion, with 'effects' which would at all times call down deprecation from purists and with a new organ—an instrument to which he was fondly attached. There is Handel anxious for 'exactness' in performance—by implication rhythmic precision (the 'beating time' suggests that Handel was ahead of his period in conducting technique, although he would appear to have preferred direction from the keyboard) and there is Handel 'overstocked with money'. Those who rashly and falsely laid bankruptcy at his door in the previous year could not have noted Jennens's remark. Jennens would have been affronted had he known that his posthumous fame was to depend on his sporadic bouts of co-operation with Handel. He felt himself to be more important than has the judgement of posterity. But then he was rich, his wealth having been inherited from industrial (and industrious) ancestors who helped to lay the foundations of Birmingham commerce. The combination of wealth, leisure, and ostentation leads to dubious artistic integrity. Jennens, therefore, chiefly distinguished himself by expressing opinions on literature which won the opprobrium of professional scholars. On the other hand he was concerned with three of the finest libretti with which Handel had to deal. *Saul, Israel in Egypt,* and *Messiah.* The two former belonged to the same year.

Saul was commenced on July 3, 1738 and completed on September 27. Four days later *Israel in Egypt* was started. The composition of this oratorio took twenty-seven days. Or perhaps we should add the nights as well, for when

Handel had a work on the stocks he allowed himself little ease until the end was reached.

The *London Daily Post* of January 3, 1739 gave this information to its readers:

We hear that, on Tuesday se'ennight, the King's Theatre [in the Haymarket] will be opened with a new oratorio, composed by Mr Handel, called *Saul*. The pit and boxes will be put together. The tickets delivered on Monday the 15th, and Tuesday 16th (the day of performance), at half a guinea each. Gallery, 5s. The gallery will be opened at 4; the pit and boxes at 5. To begin at 6 o'clock.

Saul, viewed from this distance of time, appears as the most epic work produced, up to that time, in English music. *Israel in Egypt* is even more monumental, but it is without the balance and proportion of the companion work. In viewing *Israel in Egypt* we are, as it were, seeing a sculpture as of Praxiteles or Scopas in partial mutilation. The suggestion, on which Handel acted, that arias should be introduced, was a sound one. The state of high tension within the drama and the massiveness of the architecture both call for relief and additional arias must add variety to this mainly choral work as does the Gothic screening over Romanesque in Gloucester.

After the breakdown of 1737 Handel was inclined to dark introspection. *Saul*, as we have discovered, is a painful drama: *Israel in Egypt* has the prime requirement of Aristotelian tragedy—it is an imitation 'of events inspiring fear or pity'. The issues involved are larger than those which are merely personal in origin. It is the study of a people. In parenthesis it may be included that fortuitous circumstance (or was it entirely fortuitous?) directs, in retrospect, attention to the application of the universal to the particular. Great art always leads from one to the other and back again to implement the belief that the background of apprehensible reality is a greater and mostly incomprehensible reality. 1739, again we notice a parallel with the events of two centuries later, was the year in which the storm-cloud of war burst. A superficial enthusiasm for a 'righteous' war against a reviled enemy could hardly have exorcized the general fear—epigramatically expressed by Walpole—of the unforeseeable consequences of warfare. 'Madam', said the Prime Minister to the Queen, 'they are now ringing their bells: they will soon be wringing their hands.' *Israel in Egypt* has as foundation the tribulation of a race. Deliverance comes, but the thought of the agony remains. Thanksgiving therefore, is heartfelt.

For some reason or other Handel wrote the second part of this oratorio first. That he turned back to furnish the prologue may be taken as indicative of his general capacity for seeing any biblical plot against its larger background.

Between *Saul* and *Israel in Egypt* lies one obvious connection. Both works move between C minor and C major. Because the basis of eighteenth century music was clarity in definition the key selection appears of fundamental importance. C minor was for Handel—as later for Beethoven—the setting for tragedy. On the whole this key is used sparingly: it is avoided in the keyboard music, in the organ concertos, infects only one of the concerti grossi and stands in the oratorios in notable isolation. The two works under present discussion are most generously imbued with that colour. But elsewhere choruses of lamentation and of mourning similarly emphasize their character. In *Esther* there is 'Ye sons of Israel, mourn'; in *Judas Maccabaeus* 'Mourn ye afflicted'; in *Jephtha* 'How dark, O Lord, are thy decrees'; and in *Messiah*—and here lies the real climax of the tragedy of mankind—'He trusted in God'.

A minimum of reading will reveal to the student that a proportion of Handel is, in fact, not Handel at all. *Israel in Egypt* (this is the generally accepted point of view, although on the other side there is ingeniously adduced evidence) is an anthology, drastically edited by Handel, of Stradella (*Il Barcheggio*), Kerl (*Modulatio Organica super Magnificat*), Erba (*Magnificat*), Urio (*Te Deum*), and early Handel. Hunting

the Stradella was, as we have seen, an engaging occupation
in the seventeenth century and it has proved so ever since:
Kerl, Urio and others are additional hares who have provided sport for sharp-nosed musicological hounds. After
following the field several times with Sedley Taylor and
Robinson one is forced to the conclusion that no final
conclusions can be drawn regarding the major allegations of
plagiarism. Though none of this is likely to disturb the
musician *pur sang*. *Israel in Egypt* is a work of art whatever
the quarries from which its material may have been brought.

Jeremy Taylor was moved to write—his composition like
that of Handel welled out from a sympathetic and imaginative love for his fellow men—'What an infinite number of
slaves and beggars, of persecuted and oppressed people,
fill all the corners of the earth with groans, and heaven itself
with weeping prayers and sad remembrances'. Handel's
first chorus is a transcription of this observation.

In its stage management this chorus is thrilling in its
emergence. First the contraltos of the second choir: then
the women of both choirs—in unison (T. S. Eliot feels the
same sense of marked melancholy in *Murder in the Cathedral*):
then sopranos and tenors: then added contraltos. At bar
23 the basses—this holding back of what we know is to
come is tremendous in effect—enter with this statement:

29.

The double choir is employed in this oratorio because
it represents the vast assembly of the children of Israel
and, secondarily, of the whole of humanity. From beginning

G

to end this oratorio is a dramatic *tour de force*. The first chorus, superficially less obvious in its painting than later choruses, gives us onomatopoeically the sighs of the afflicted; the deep waters of discontent move to an inexorable 6/4 rhythm; burdens are laid (and particularly on the sopranos) in the form of high notes adhering to awkward syllables; an illusion of antiquity is gained by an occasional glance at Phrygian modality.

The plagues are famously interpreted in a variety of realistic impressions, which have extracted more recently that mild contempt which springs from ignorance of intention. Handel, and most composers of his period, were expected to simulate reality. Therefore if the frogs hopped, if the insects buzzed (since they aptly do so in the strings of the orchestra this only comes off if chorus and orchestra meet on equal terms: no contemporary band can set us scratching if hundreds and hundreds of singers divert us from the mosquito motive), if the hailstones rattled, if the thick darkness crept phantasmagorically over the landscape so much the better. Now one must expect to be entertained by Handel's frogs (frogs are in general entertaining creatures) and shattered by his hailstones. And choral singers, or rather their conductors, must see to it that they achieve—by precision, variety of tone, dramatic sense, and by mentally viewing the picture passing through the music—the touch of *verismo* which makes Handel a harbinger of romanticism.

In the hailstone chorus we encounter the brilliance of inspired simplicity—there is little else than tonic and dominant—but in the darkness music we have, by way of contrast:

30.

He sent a thick dark-ness, o-ver all the land, o-ver

all   the   land,   e - ven   dark - ness   which might be   felt:

than which *Tristan und Isolde* has nothing more effectively nomadic in stealthy modulation. The plague music is bordered on either side by fugues borrowed from the set of six which Handel wrote in 1720 and published in 1735. The first, 'They loathed to drink of the river', is excellent as introduction to the scene. It is minatory in that its subject (c.f. 'And with his stripes', also the 'Kyrie' from the Mozart *Requiem*) was an accepted symbol of the horrific, but it is not overpowering in emotional significance. It forms the first stage in an emotional crescendo just as 'He smote all the first-born of Egypt' is the last. The fugal choruses throughout stand as relief, as points of relative neutrality from which excursions to other fields may easily and quickly be effected. From 'He smote all the first-born of Egypt' we proceed to consideration of the Israelites, now at last impressed with the prospect of a fairer future.

So the sunshine of Handel's geniality irradiates 'But as for his people', a chorus which rides with elegance and charm to a more or less emphatic conclusion, the plain triads set in homophonic rigour declaiming that 'there was not one feeble person among their tribes'. And then—after a fugal exposition of the Egyptians' relief at their departure—the Red Sea is dried up. Elsewhere plain recitative might have served to state this fact. But the miracle is too overwhelming for such baldness of expression. The chorus, therefore, is used and in the brief grandeur of 'He rebuked the Red Sea' we see the immensity of the awe which descended on all who were present. Later in the work this quasi-recitative treatment occurs again, but with nothing like the same power.

A reference back to the Chandos anthem 'The Lord is my light' introduces a sea motif in 'But the waters overwhelmed their enemies'. Herein the billows in the bass (a little conjuring and we arrive at *La Cathédrale engloutie*) overwhelm not only the enemies of the Israelites but also the choir, who are engaged in somewhat dull and negligent narrative. But it should be remembered that Handel was not averse sometimes from allowing his orchestra precedence over his singers. Besides, we should know the Chandos anthem in which the same figuration preludes 'It is the Lord that ruleth the seas'.

The second part of *Israel in Egypt* (in reality the first part to be written) is more truthfully an extended hymn of praise than an act for an oratorio, but no choral work in existence has a greater termination than lies here in 'Sing ye to the Lord'. We have the apogee of musical pageantry and, more than mere display, 'the feeling of multitudinous movement, of infinite cavalcades filing off, and the tread of innumerable armies'.

Israel in Egypt, however, was not a success. Neither the addition of the music of the Funeral Anthem of the previous year (which Handel was determined to use again somewhere, even though he had tried, but failed, to fit it into *Saul*) nor of Italian ballads, given to la Francesina, saved the oratorio from disapproval.

A letter in the *Daily Post* for April 13 (the oratorio had been performed on April 4 and 11 and was to be done again on April 17) gives a contemporary view of the situation:

Upon my arrival in town three days ago, I was not a little surprised to find that Mr Handel's last oratorio, *Israel in Egypt*, which had been performed but once, was advertized to be for the last time on Wednesday. I was almost tempted to think that his genius had failed him; but must own myself agreeably disappointed. I was not only pleased but also affected by it; for I never met with any musical performance in which the words and sentiments were so thoroughly studied, and so clearly understood; and as the words are taken from the Bible, they are perhaps some of the most sublime parts of it. I was indeed

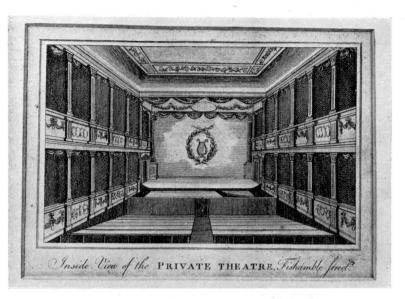

Inside View of the PRIVATE THEATRE, *Fishamble street.*

The *interior of Neale's Music Hall, Dublin;*
after adaptation as a private theatre

concerned that so excellent a work of so great a genius was neglected, for though it was a polite and attentive audience, it was not large enough, I doubt, to encourage him in any future attempt. As I should be extremely sorry to be deprived of hearing this again, and found many of the auditors in the same disposition, yet, being afraid Mr Handel will not undertake it without some publick encouragement, because he may think himself precluded by his advertizement (that it was to be the last time), I beg leave, by your means, to convey, not only my own, but the desires of several others, that he will perform this again some time next week.

Chapter Six

MESSIAH

MESSIAH is in a number of ways emblematic of escapist philosophy. For Handel it meant release from the cruder realism of operatic definitiveness, and from the similar narrative tendencies of representational oratorio; it meant, further, absorption in a series of purely spiritual problems. It is, therefore, an essay vastly different both in invention and execution from anything that had previously been achieved. It is unique, but the quality of the uniqueness is not always understood.

For our contemporary audience, and indeed for almost any audience at any time, *Messiah* affords opportunity for temporary escape to things of the spirit, relief from the burden of deliberate and materialist thought and a sure catharsis of sentimental emotion. There is a difference between our form of escape and that of Handel. He turned aside to wrestle with difficulties which only seldom came to the forefront of his mind; we, for the most part, eliminate the logic of the inspired thesis and seize on those fragments which set in train associated ideas of familiar proportion and desirable shape. In so far as this happens there is nothing to which Handel, whose mind continually anticipated the thought of Shelley that 'a poem is the very image of life expressed in its eternal truth', would have taken exception. But he would have protested against an attitude incapable of synthesizing the parts into the whole. *Messiah* is an epic and as such rises to a higher level than do any of the separate episodes. *Messiah* to Handel was as philosophically conclusive as the ninth symphony to Beethoven. For us does it suggest more than a *pasticcio* of scenes—charming, tragic, dignified or what you will? Is it greater in significance than its sentimental place in the Christmas or Easter holidays allows? Is not the total appreciation of the English summarized by Lamb (a notable Handel addict)?

In confessing ourselves lovers of all the pride, pomp, and circumstance of glorious Christmas, indoors and out of doors, parties, plum-puddings, pantomimes, holly boughs, galanty shows, wassail-bowls, forfeits, mistletoe, and all thereunto belonging we hold it no unreasonable intrusion of the sentimental to add that we love to lie awake at night, in the intervals of our gaieties, and listen to those mysteriously denominated persons, the waits; always provided, that the performance of the bass is not totally ignorant of that part of his art. We have a tender recollection of the homely Christmas carol, that used to be sung at school; nor can we hear, without particular emotion at this season, that divine composition of Handel's, with the recitative full of singleness of purpose and a truly pastoral simplicity, 'There were shepherds abiding in the fields'.

The detachment of any one number (or section) from its context in this work is doubly indefensible: on the one hand Handel's method was always towards musical synthesis—towards the symphonic ideal; on the other he was herein developing an argument—an *argumentum ad deum*. The mind of genius tends to work cyclically. In *Messiah* we witness the inception of a new cycle: Handel turning from contemplation of life to consideration of the justification of life. The conclusion of his argument is this—*Christus orbis redemptor*.

In order to compose *Messiah* Handel needed to escape in more senses than one. He needed to escape from himself (of all his works this, strangely, is the least Handelian), from his poetasters, the text standing in the sublime austerity of our Jacobean translators, and from his environment. *Messiah* was written for performance in Dublin. It is worth recollection that Faulkner's *Dublin Journal* (April 6-10, 1742), in an advertisement, indicates an *ad hoc* origin. 'Many Ladies and Gentlemen who are well-wishers to this Noble and Grand Charity for which this Oratorio was composed. . . .' There is no reason to dispute the literal interpretation of this clause. Dubourg, leader of the Irish Court band, was an old friend of Handel. The music of Handel had featured very prominently in the programmes of the Dublin and Charitable Musical Society and many there were in the Irish capital to bless the unknown benefactor whose music had, in a practical manner of speaking, proved their redemption.

Music performed by the Anglo-Irish aristocracy of the city had 'enlarged the fund for the reception of sick and wounded poor of this kingdom into Dr Steven's Hospital in Werburgh Street': the Charitable Infirmary, opened in 1728 at Inns' Quay (where now stand the Four Courts) and the Mercer's Hospital, founded in 1734, had benefited from annual performances at St Andrew's Church; 'great numbers of poor confined Debtors in the several Jayles of this City, have this Week been discharged by the Charity and Contributions raised by Members of the Charitable and Musical Society held in Fishamble Street'. (*Dublin News-Letter*, December 29—January 2, 1741-2).

Regarding Handel, and speaking of the Mercer's Hospital, the Charitable Infirmary, the Lying-In Hospital, and the Hospital for Incurables, Townshend writes, 'Perhaps the works of no other composer have so largely contributed to the relief of human suffering, as those of this illustrious musician'. His works were the staple fare of the Dubliners and the respect accorded to him was partially intended for one aspect, and that the most encouraging, of his class and his generation—the zeal for philanthropy which led to the faith in practice of General Oglethorpe, Captain Coram, the founders of the Irish and English hospitals and Handel, as benefactor of the Foundlings, himself.

From one point of view the chosen text of *Messiah* comes, literally, to life. 'Comfort ye, my people, saith your God';

'and they that dwell in the land of the shadow of death, upon them hath the light shined'; 'Then shall the eyes of the blind be opened, and the ears of the deaf unstopped; then shall the lame man leap as a hart, and the tongue of the dumb shall sing'; '. . . and gently lead them that are with young'; 'And with his stripes we are healed'; 'Let us break their bonds asunder'; 'Even so in Christ shall all be made alive'; 'Death is swallowed up in victory': in all these there is relevance to the charities of particular concern to the Dubliners. If it be objected that this is entirely fortuitous it should be remembered that more than once Handel made topical allusions. There is the pointed chorale quotation in the Funeral Anthem, the nature of the *Occasional Oratorio*, the sensitiveness to current affairs in the specifically Jewish-heroic oratorios, the aptness of the Foundling Hospital Anthem and the character of *Solomon*. Further it should be emphasized that the eighteenth century philosophy of music, backed as it was by the pervasive influence of the opera, was contained within the thesis of mimesis. Delany unconsciously underlined the connection between music and life when the collison of Mrs Cibber's reputation with her performance of 'He was despised' brought forth, it is reported, the decanal ejaculation 'Woman, for this thy sins be forgiven thee'.

There are other possible pointers to the sources of inspiration. Pope had in 1712 published his *Messiah* (N.B. *not The Messiah*). Certain of the passages from Isaiah fall also into Handel's scheme and quite clearly propose a theme for musical treatment. Although Handel was, by no stretch of the imagination, a religious man (except that he behaved consistently as a Christian should) he had the Pastor of Giebichenstein, his maternal grandfather and the strong theological influence of the university of Halle in the background. The relative solemnity of *Messiah* and the particular sections which speak in terms of Teutonic homophony recall these antecedents. We also remember that a quarter of a century before, Handel had written his most severe music in the traditional *Passion* format.

Thus far we are assured of this: that Handel had solid reasons for writing this work and that these reasons happened to coincide with his inclination—he had reached the disillusioned end of his career of operatic impresario—to withdraw from the rout of London life.

At this point we may turn aside from an examination of principles to more mundane facts. Handel's habit of rapid construction came less from the supposed mystery of 'inspiration' than from the fluency of technique: with him a set piece was accomplished in the shortest possible time so that other aspects of life could be accommodated. *Messiah* was composed, with perhaps rather more than usual haste, between August 22 and September 14, 1741. Clearly the beginning of the season of mellow fruitfulness. The admirable Jennens, admirable if only because he in some way or other provoked genius to expression on more than one occasion, collaborated in the selection and arrangement of the words. The original score comprises some 250 pages of manuscript; which means that Handel wrote, on the average, a little over ten pages a day. If it is at all possible to estimate the progress of the work it would appear that the work *might* just have been achieved within the not unreasonable limits of a seven hour day (that is, counting in Sundays). The autograph is evidence of very rapid performance and, it should be remembered, Handel had the advantage of having some of his material previously to hand; 'And he shall purify', 'For unto us', 'His yoke is easy', 'All we like sheep', 'Hallelujah', are remodelled Italian duets; 'And with His stripes' is a conventional fugue on an already familiar subject, 'The Lord gave the word' carries the 'busy hum' of *L'Allegro* a stage further, the Pastoral Symphony is in easy imitation of Corelli; it may additionally be supposed with some certainty that other sketches, either actual or mental, were only awaiting transcription. In case credulity still assigns to Handel what was added to him by Mozart (and others) it should be mentioned that his orchestral score was slight and that many of the arias carried above the bass and the solo part only a single violin line.

The finished score, not a model of neatness, went from Handel to his old friend and secretary, J. C. Smith. He prepared the conducting score (now at Tenbury) for the Dublin performance and superintended the copying of the parts. Thereafter came other scores, each in detail differing from its predecessor; one which eventually came to the Hamburg City library, one to the Goldschmidt collection, one to the Fitzwilliam Museum, and one, a posthumous copy, to the Foundling Hospital. In 1894 Dr Davan Wetton discovered at the Foundling Hospital the wind parts originally used there. Such is the material on which the editor must work. The variety in detail, to be discussed later, indicates the hopelessness of attempting a definitive edition to enable an authentic and irreproachable replica of an 'original' performance. (Not that the attempt to represent Handel in something approximate to eighteenth century form is not incumbent on the conscientious and imaginative conductor!) Handel changed his mind according to the varying circumstances under which he had to work. He wrote and amended always with an occasion in mind. His achievement was also, in part, the achievement of his co-partners. Music was then essentially a team activity, Handel the captain, with frequent ideas about changing the bowling.

Several localities in England and Ireland have developed legends about the countryside responsible for the 'inspiration' of *Messiah*. A man once instructed me in a train that a certain house in Staffordshire had harboured the 'master' as he poured out 'the immortal strains'. In fact the house—Bernard Granville's at Calwich—was not then built, although Handel was a guest there in later years. Other legends exist. One, which may stand for all, is dealt with by Townshend. This also shows the extent of Handel's extra-inspirational activities. We are told how, in Dublin, Handel visited Alexander Lee, the music-seller on Corkhill. 'A gentleman', writes Townshend, 'has told me that when he was a boy, he heard Mr Lee (then a very old man) affirm that Handel composed the *Messiah* in his house on Cork-hill, and that he had seen him in the act of writing it.' What Handel was doing (Lee was clearly oblivious of the rehearsal in Chester on the eve of departure for Ireland) was correcting copyist's errors.

Handel arrived in Dublin, from Chester and via Holyhead, on November 18, 1741. For the benefit of sightseers, the Chester rehearsal had taken place at the Golden Falcon (now reduced in status from tavern to tea-shop) in Bridge Street. The business capacity of Handel may be gauged from the fact that on December 5 *Faulkner's Journal* advertised, for the new Music Hall in Fishamble Street, a series of six subscription concerts. These, on December 23, January 13 and 27, February 3 and 10, included *L'Allegro*, *Acis and Galatea*, *Ode for St Cecilia's Day*, *Esther* and various concertos. After these another series followed, by request. On February 17 and March 2 Hibernian enthusiasm was raised to a higher level by *Alexander's Feast*. The succeeding concerts, March 17, 29 and 31 and April 7, provided *L'Allegro*, the popularity of which speaks volumes for the eclectic taste of the public, *Hymen* (a concert-room abstract of the penultimate opera) and *Esther*. Concertos, without or with organ, abounded in this unique sequence of celebration.

Handel comments rapturously on the quality of his supporters—'Bishops, Deans, Heads of the Colledge, the most eminent People in the Law as the Chancellor, Auditor General, etc., etc.' He would have approved the 'land of saints and scholars' appellation.

The musical society which instigated these events supplied not only money and administrative ability, but also musical talent. This latter was in general under the preliminary direction of Dubourg or, Irishly, Duburk.

Handel's life in Dublin stands in busy profile. One can see the daily stream of callers at his lodgings in Abbey Street, some to ask for favours—'Ordered that Messrs Portland, Owen . . . and Wynne . . . be and are desired to wait on Mr Handel to ask the favour of him to play on the Organ at the Musical Performances in St Andrew's Church'; some in response to advertisements announcing the disposal of tickets for the subscription concerts; some to rehearse, for Handel was in the habit of promoting sectional rehearsals at home; and some, like Mrs Vernon and Dr Quin, simply to gossip. Out of the house there were many attractions: the theatre, the sights of the city and the surrounding country, concerts and the races at the Curragh. Perhaps Handel missed the races but one cannot imagine him forgoing the Theatre Royal, where, on a night in January, 'was acted the celebrated Masque of Comus. Written by the sublime Milton [much in Handel's thoughts at this time], and now adapted for the stage. The Part of Comus by Mr Quin, Lady by Mrs Cibber, And the Character of Euphrosyne and Sabrina . . . performed by Madam Chateauneuf, with the original Musick, and all the Decorations proper to the Mask'.

On a later date and after the first *Messiah* performances there was at Fishamble Street

. . . a grand Concert of Musick, by Mr Charles the Hungarian [this was a cosmopolitan society], Master of the French Horn, with his Second, accompanied by all the best Hands in this City—First Act, 1. An Overture with French Horns, called now Pastor Fido. 2 The 6th Concerto of Signior Geminiani. 3 A Solo on the French Horn by Mr Charles to shew the beauty of that Instrument. 4 A Concerto on the Clarinet. Second Act. 1. Mr Handel's Water Musick, with the March in Scipio, and the grand Chorus in Atalanta. 2 A Concerto on the German Flute, by Mr Lavieux. 3 A Solo on the Hautbois de Amour [*sic*], by Mr Charles. 4 Signior Hasse's Concerto with Signior Barbarini's Minuet. Third Act 1 The Overture in Saul, with the Dead March, composed by Mr Handel, but never performed here before. 2 A Select Piece on the Shalamo. 3 A Solo on the Violoncello, by Signior Pasqualino. 4 The Turkish Music in the original Taste, as

performed at the Spring Gardens, Vauxhall, London.—N.B. The Clarinet, the Hautbois d'Amour, and Shalamo, were never heard in this
Kingdom before.

All of which, demonstrating nascent romanticism in the
Turkish music and the new awareness of orchestral colour
possibilities, was good value for 5/5 and of considerable
interest to Handel who, of all composers, was the most ready
to appraise novelty in musical expression.

Indeed he was rapidly, if report can be trusted, becoming
hibernior hiberniis. 'Handel', writes Townshend, 'is said to
have declared that he would willingly assign the fame he had
acquired by his most celebrated compositions, for the glory
of being the inventor of the air *Aileen Aroon*.' Or again in
respect of the lost *Forest Music*—'In the second movement,
which is in 6/8 time, there is a remarkable blending of the
character of Irish music with the peculiar style of Handel'.
And in the Fitzwilliam Museum there is, in Handel's
autograph, a copy of an Irish folk song.

The build-up of *Messiah* was magnificent. Handel, like a
touring cricketer, played himself in, established himself in
public affection by reciprocating courtesy and hospitality
and accordingly proved a more magnetic influence than at
any time since his first visits to Italy and London. The
authorities found events sometimes almost embarrassing
but, being Ireland, a little inconvenience was willingly
endured. In the *Dublin News-Letter* (January 12-16) we find
what must surely be the first suggestion of one-way traffic.
'Gentlemen and Ladies are desired to order their Coaches
and Chairs to come down Fishamble Street, which will
prevent a great deal of Inconveniences that happen'd the
Night before.' When *Messiah* was performed ladies left
their hoops, gentlemen their swords at home and at the
summer performance some of the window panes were
temporarily withdrawn in order to prevent asphyxiation.

On April 8 a public rehearsal of *Messiah* took place. The
result of this was that the *Faulkner's Journal* proclaimed this

to be 'the finest composition of Musick that ever was heard'. On April 13 was the first public performance, admirably reported in three Dublin papers thus:

On Tuesday last, Mr Handel's sacred grand oratorio, *The Messiah*, was performed in the New Music Hall in Fishamble Street; the best judges allowed it to be the most finished piece of music. Words are wanting to express the exquisite delight it afforded to the admiring crowded audience. The sublime, the grand, and the tender, adapted to the most elevated, majestic, and moving words, conspired to transport and charm the ravished heart and ear. It is but justice to Mr Handel that the world should know he generously gave the money arising from this grand performance to be equally shared by the Society for Relieving Prisoners, the Charitable Infirmary, and Mercer's Hospital, for which they will ever gratefully remember his name; and that the gentlemen of the two choirs, Mr Dubourg, Mrs Avolio and Mrs Cibber, who all performed their parts to admiration, acted also on the same disinterested principle, satisfied with the deserved applause of the public, and the conscious pleasure of promoting such useful and extensive charity. There were above seven hundred people in the room, and the sum collected for that noble and pious charity amounted to about £400, out of which £127 goes to each of the three great and pious charities.

Mr L. Whyte in the *Faulkner's Journal* (April 17-20) was less objective and set the pace for the pietistic Handel neophyte of the future.

> *What can we offer more in* Handel's *praise?*
> *Since his* Messiah *gain'd him Groves of Bays;*
> *Groves that can neither wither nor decay,*
> *When Visto's his Ability display;*
> *Here Nature smiles, when fac'd with Handel's art,*
> *Transports the ear and ravishes the Heart;*
> *To all the nobler* Passions *we are mov'd,*
> *When various strains repeated and improv'd,*
> *Express each different Circumstance and State,*
> *As if each Sound became articulate.*
>   *None but the Great* Messiah *could inflame,*
> *And raise his Soul to so Sublime a* Theme,
> *Profound the Thoughts, the Subject all divine,*

Not like the Tales of Pindus and the Nine:
O, Heathen Deities, those Sons of Fiction,
Sprung from old Fables, stuff'd with Contradiction,
But our Messiah, blessed be his Name!
Both Heaven and Earth his Miracles proclaim,
His Birth, his Passion, and his Resurrection,
With his Ascension have a strong connection;
What prophets spoke, or Sybels cou'd relate,
In time were all these Prophecies compleat
The Word made Flesh, both God and Man became;
Then let all nations glorify his Name,
Let Hallelujahs' round the Globe be sung,
To our Messiah, from a Virgin sprung.

Mr Whyte set out to applaud Mr Handel and finished by producing a third-rate tract. Many observations on Handel since that time have sprung from tractarian minds.

The music of the oratorio is a vehicle for words. It is, therefore amenable to the general import of the words. But also it exists in its own right. The first consideration is, perhaps, the architecture of the music, in which the key word is homogeneity. *Messiah* is, indeed, the most homogeneous of all Handel's larger works (this is the valid title to supremacy, if the argument regarding priority among superlatives is worth the pursuit) and the secret of this lies in the interrelation of aria and recitative and the logical disposition of key centres. With regard to the recitatives it will be noticed that they have more claim to tunefulness than is often the case, while the arias are comparatively modest in adornment. It is generally assumed that criticism of *Messiah* is indicative of imbecility. Sir John Hawkins was unpopular when he observed that the 'airs . . . are greatly inferior to most of those in Handel's Operas, and other Oratorios'. And yet Hawkins was not far wrong. Nor was Jennens when he expressed the opinion that Handel might have done better. Within limits Handel, from the point of view of the fashionable eighteenth century, might have done better. He might have been more demonstrative, but Handel's judicious, though anachronistic conclusion was that exhibitionism would be out of place. This sobriety spreads also to the orchestration, which is throughout restrained.

But there is a wealth of subtle colouring in another direction. The contrasts of tonality are masterly. In each *scena* (the parts may surely be thus mentally subdivided, bearing in mind long experience of the division of opera plots) Handel effects a localized consistency with colour and climax. From the grey E minor of the overture we progress through the striking juxtaposition of E major to the inevitability of A major. This brings us to that moment of first climax when the chorus enters. Next a respectful and awesome minor section, for this is the preparation in the first Advent for the God of Old Testament power and punishment and purification. But the true Christian God comes in other guise; therefore the levitation of the D major—G major axis with 'O Thou that tellest' at one end and 'For unto us' at the other. The pastoral culmination shines lambently in major tonality.

Part the Second opens, appropriately, in the minor, though Handel's power in making a major key sound infinite in pathos twice occurs. A major key for 'All we like sheep' together with the exhilaration of rhythm is surprising. Or is it? Handel never, even in *Messiah*, forgetful of pointed reference indicates an enjoyment in sinful behaviour as common as it may be reprehensible. Or is this fancy? Somehow when we turn the corner into the fierce psychology of 'He trusted in God', I feel not. To the end of this part of the oratorio interest and therefore key mutation is widely dispersed. One point particularly to be noticed is the effect of running from the second section of 'Why do the heathen' straight into 'Let us break their bonds asunder'. A baseless convention adds to the former a *da capo* which Handel particularly wished to avoid. In no version is a *da capo* indicated: accordingly we must not

H

presume to correct Handel. The chorus *is* the third part, balancing in key the opening, albeit the melodic material is different. The dramatic, as distinct from the musical, value of maintaining what the composer wrote gives us the energetic call to arms supervening on a reflection on tyranny.

The third part of *Messiah* is a *lobgesang*—an extension of the finale of *Esther*, in dignified and ecclesiastically minded exultation. The predominant key (on acount of the trumpets) is D major, for which we have been prepared by the antecedent 'Hallelujah'.

On May 29, 1784, Dr Burney heard *Messiah* in the Handel Commemoration in Westminster Abbey. His opinions on the work—and the performance—are valuable in that he was brought up under direct Handelian influence. He had, as a boy, seen Handel in Chester in 1741 and in later years he had attended many rehearsals directed by Handel. When, therefore, we read Burney we read the judgement of one who was observing a masterpiece of his own period. It is certainly to our advantage to go back beyond the romantic mists and to appreciate Handel from an eighteenth century angle.

In respect of the overture:

In order therefore to suppress every idea of levity in so sacred [here Burney anticipates] a performance as the Messiah, he very judiciously finished the Overture without an Air. And the short symphony to the accompanied Recitative, or *Aria parlante*, '*Comfort ye my people*' . . . seems to such as are not acquainted with the Oratorio, a preparation for the light minuet, gavot, or jig, with which Overtures are usually terminated; but how exquisitely are judicious ears disappointed! Indeed, I am acquainted with no movement of the same cast, to the words of any language, which is more grateful and soothing than this. There is not a note, either in the principal melody or accompaniment that is become vulgar, common, or unmeaning.

To pass on to the high lights, as they appeared to Burney, we come to :

There is a very curious expression of the words attempted in the Air: 'The people who walked in darkness have seen a great light ' . . .

where the chromatic and indeterminate modulation seems to delineate the uncertain footsteps of persons exploring their way in obscurity.

Handel's fugal writing appealed consistently and chiefly on account of its clarity but of 'For unto us a child is born' he comments 'There is poetry of the highest class in the Music, as well as the words'. This contains a moral: counterpoint is ideally an emanation of feeling rather than of rarified ratiocination. Handel was as emotional as any Romantic but more subtle in definition. Burney saw the shades of subtlety. So that when he comes to the Pastoral Symphony he rhapsodizes over the simplicity of effect thus: '[It], played without wind-instruments by violins only, in the most subdued manner, was balmy and delicious! The pianos or whispers of such multiplied sounds produced a sweetness of so new and exquisite a kind, that the musical *technica* furnishes no terms adequate to their effects.'

The *Gloria*, over which—with trumpets, expressly marked, *da lontano e un poco piano*—the theatrical genius presides, caught from Burney this curious statement: 'There is more *claire obscure* in this short Chorus than perhaps had ever been attempted at the time it was composed.'

Part II is self-explanatory and Burney says very much what we would say without premeditation of the successive movements—'the single stamp of solemnity', the 'highest idea of excellence in pathetic expression'. In this vein we arrive at 'And with his stripes' of which the nature is compared with that of the music of the sixteenth century. 'This fugue . . . may fairly be compared with movements of the same kind in Palestrina, Tallis, and Bird, which, in variety, it very much surpasses.' It is a far cry to the early masters but, none the less, Burney does touch truth in indicating the deep-set antiquity in Handel's outlook. In other places, not, perhaps in this German school fugue, the contact with the living tradition of the English church is apparent. Sixteenth century music was more real than a library acquaintance would allow.

'He trusted in God' contains in its words 'the triumphal insolence' and is prophetic of 'the contumelious language of the Jews during the crucifixion of our Saviour . . . Handel has given [the words] the effect, not of the taunts and presumption of an individual, but the scoffs and scorns of a confused multitude.' George III thought this movement notable for its genius in expression and it was he who reminded Dr Burney that frequently Handel would take the subject of this fugue and run into extemporizations of 'the most sublime ideas, and wonderful sallies of imagination'.

Handel wears learning lightly at all times and attention is drawn to this fact in the construction of the delicious and airy chorus (alas! that it should ever be 'cut') 'Let all the angels of God', 'in what ancient theorists called *minor Prolation*; in which the reply to a subject given, though in similar intervals, is made in notes of different value'. It is diminution of the subject which gives to the chorus its sense of aspiration. The Hallelujah chorus overwhelmed Burney the critic. He regarded it as 'the triumph of Handel, of the Commemoration, and of the musical art'. Fitzgerald, who was behind no man in regard for Handel, preserves a balance unique in addressing this item. It is, he says, 'a chorus, not of angels, but of well-fed earthly choristers, ranged tier above tier in a Gothic cathedral, with princes for audience. . . . .' But Burney drives home one implication which might appear to be of theological or philosophical significance: 'And finally, the words—"King of Kings, and Lord of Lords" always set to a single sound, which seems to stand at bay, while the other parts attack it in every possible manner. . . .' What we hear is Handel acknowledging at this point his certainty of the impregnability of the rock.

Handel, as has already been remarked, changed his ideas in detail. Some of the changes are of relatively minor concern (except for the musicologist), but two major changes of intention may be extracted for notice. In the original autograph the aria 'Rejoice greatly' runs fluidly in 12/8 time,

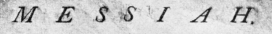

MESSIAH.

AN

ORATORIO

Compos'd by Mr. *HANDEL*.

MAJORA CANAMUS.

*And without Controversy, great is the Mystery of Godliness :
God was manifested in the Flesh, justified by the Spirit
seen of Angels, preached among the Gentiles, believed on in
the World, received up in Glory.
In whom are hid all the Treasures of Wisdom and Knowledge.*

DUBLIN: Printed by George Faulkner, 1742.

(*Price a British Six-pence.*)

Title page of the Word Book of Messiah: Dublin 1742

but almost immediately (see the Dublin score) the sharper edged version with the familiar semiquavers was substituted. As an individual song the original draft is, to my mind, preferable; Handel, however, considering the part in relation to the whole estimated that more variety would be imparted if the four-square setting were substituted, there being frequent reference to the rhythmic idea of the siciliano throughout the oratorio.

Another item which underwent major operations was 'How beautiful are the feet'. This commenced as an aria for soprano, with what is now the succeeding chorus ('Their sound is gone out') given as a middle section, the movement being terminated by a *da capo*. An addition to the autograph score gives the aria to contralto (in C minor) with 'Their sound is gone out' assigned, in F, to tenor. The choral setting of this latter movement is, incidentally, also bound up as an appendix to the original score.

A MS. in the Fitzwilliam Museum, a Handel autograph, gives a magnificent extension of 'How beautiful are the feet' into an alto solo with succeeding chorus. For this the text is extended '. . . glad tidings of salvation, that saith unto Zion: Thy God reigneth! Break forth into joy!' This is a magnificent movement (which might well be made available for separate use, if it can never recapture the place it once occupied in the oratorio), particularly as the choir carries into 'Their sound is gone out' with a brilliant sense of climax. This is a remodelled setting of a work originally composed for the Chapel Royal. Two other variants give us duets for two altos with chorus.

The exigencies of performance necessitated other changes. 'Comfort ye my people' has in the Dublin MS. the names of Mr Beard, Mr Lowe, and Sga Avolio pencilled in: thus the aria was on occasion given to soprano; similarly with 'Every valley'. 'But who may abide' was sometimes for bass (the original intention), sometimes for tenor (Mr Low[e]), sometimes for contralto (Guadagni) and sometimes for soprano

(Miss Young, Miss Brent, Sig. Ricciarelli, Miss Frederick). The key was altered to suit the singer. 'Rejoice greatly' was heard by 'The Boy', Frasi and Mr Beard. 'He shall feed His flock' and 'Come unto Him' varied between a duet (contralto and soprano) in F and B flat and a soprano solo, in B flat. Despite the fact that Mrs Cibber had laid particular claim to 'He was despised' in the first performance this air also was sung by soprano and tenor. 'All they that see Him', although in the tenor clef and first given to Mr Beard came at least once into Signora Avolio's province. Similarly with 'Thy rebuke'.

'Behold and see' carries the names of Mr Beard, Mr Lowe, Signori Frasi and Francesina. 'He was cut off', 'But Thou didst not leave', 'Unto which of the angels' are in the same case. 'Thou art gone up on high' alternated between bass and contralto.

The list of textual alterations, which could be lengthened almost indefinitely, indicates that in Handel's lifetime there were many performances of *Messiah*. But the work which was to become, so far as English music is concerned, the head stone in the corner was nearly rejected at the outset. Dublin was enthusiastic—Dubliners were without axes to grind—but London suspicious. Handel, in common with most men of independence and initiative, had his enemies and detractors and, as is usual, they seized on irrelevancies. In 1743 *Messiah* was given three times, as against the eight performances of *Samson;* in 1744 it was ignored completely; in 1745 it was done twice. Miss Talbot expressed the cause of ostracism: 'To be sure', she wrote to Mrs Carter, 'the play-house is an unfit place for such a solemn performance'. Lord Shaftesbury seconded this. 'Partly from the scruples some persons had entertained against carrying on such a performance in the Play-House, and partly for not entering into the genius of the composition, this capital composition was but indifferently relished.'

Although at the time of their composition Handel could

not make up his mind whether he preferred *Messiah* or *Samson*
and although at a later date he demonstrated a particular
relish for *Theodora* there can be little doubt that he held
Messiah in high esteem. It was the work which he offered
to the Foundling Hospital. This in itself supports the thesis
that charity was originally the mainspring of inspiration,
for Handel would only offer to the Hospital such works as
were apposite to its benevolent activity. On May 1, 1750
Handel 'opened' the new organ which was his gift to the
Chapel with a performance of *Messiah*; there was an exceptional audiance of 1000 and many were turned away.
Handel proposed another performance on May 15. Here we
may refer to the General Committee Minutes of the Hospital
as comment on the overcrowded performance of May 1 and
the preliminary arrangements for May 15.

A Computation was made of what Number of Persons the Chapel of
this Hospital would conveniently hold, and no greater Number of
Tickets were delivered, to hear the Performance, there on the First
Instant; but so many persons of Distinctions coming unprovided with
Tickets, caused a greater number to be admitted than were expected,
and some that had Tickets not finding room to go away: To prevent
therefore any disappointment to such persons, and for the further
Promotion of this Charity, This is to give Notice, that George
Frederick Handel Esqr has generously offered, that the sacred Oratorio
called 'Messiah' shall be performed again under his direction, in the
Chapel of this Hospital on Tuesday the 15th Instant, at 12 o'Clock at
Noon, and the Tickets delivered out, and not brought in on the 1st
instant, will be then received. And no persons whatsoever will be admitted without Tickets, which will be delivered, from Monday the 7th
to Monday the 14th Instant and not after, by the Steward at the
Hospital, at Batson's Coffee House, in Cornhill, and at White's
Chocolate House in St. James's Street, at half a Guinea Each. And
care will be taken not to deliver out more Tickets, than for the Number
of Persons the Chapel will conveniently hold.

Note, There will be no Collection; and it is hoped that no persons
will take it ill that they cannot be admitted without Tickets.

From this point forward Handel was respected not because
he was among the greatest of musicians but because he

stood among those whose compassion touched, at a sensitive period in the progress of English humanitarianism, the general conscience. It is characteristic of the English that for a donation to a 'cause' there should be a *quid pro quo*—not that this should provoke cynicism in view of what, in one way or another, was achieved; it is equally a characteristic that music should be regarded not for itself alone but for its associations. Without labouring the point the present and apparently eternal adoration of *Messiah* depends on the sense that this is a religious demonstration, but demonstrative of that effectual faith that is the apotheosis of effluent kindliness. Dr Burney memorably phrased our affection for the one side of Handel and of *Messiah* when he wrote what is still pertinent '. . . this great work has been heard in all parts of the kingdom with increasing reverence and delight; it has fed the hungry, clothed the naked, fostered the orphan, and enriched succeeding managers of Oratorios, more than any single musical production in this or any country'.

From this it will be seen that it is easy to mistake purpose. The music comes first in point of importance, the tangible effects of its performance second. Therefore if we propose to study the musical aspect of Handel's oratorios we must step out of the turgid stream of sentimentality. Which is difficult but profitable, for it is impossible for the vitality of art to persist through the overlay of two centuries of irrelevent decoration.

Chapter Seven

SAMSON

AS in a large family there are among the members different groups, so the children of Handel's imagination divide according to temperament. *Saul* and *Samson*, for instance, have a good deal in common; and so have *Israel in Egypt* and *Messiah*. The two former works are interrogatory—'What is man that Thou art mindful of him?' the latter affirmatory—'I know that my Redeemer liveth' and unless this philosophic preoccupation is realized, the range of Handel's art is circumscribed by the limits of conventional pietism and, a close ally, hedonism. Handel had a good deal both of piety and hedonism (thus he appeals to those who otherwise would count themselves among the unmusical) but these qualities are merely incidental. Incidental, in the case of the philosophic oratorios, to contemplation of the abiding question of the relationship of God to man. When Handel's philosophic sensibility is admitted, his interest in Milton can be understood and, in the light of this interest, the stature of *Samson* as a work of art can more readily be recognized. It is, in more senses than one, Miltonic.

Against the fact that many libretti of Handel's setting were undistinguished from a literary point of view, must be set the reluctance of poets of competence to allow their style partially to be dictated by a musician. (Jennens protested against the composer's cavalier treatment of his libretto and

Morell once showed signs of taking umbrage on this account.) There was another factor which should be remembered when the quality of the oratorio libretto is called in question. Ready-made texts, whether for opera or oratorio, were non-existent, presumably because their composition was, from the poet's angle, non-remunerative. Handel was, however, inclined to discriminate so long as he could still observe the proprieties of oratorio performance, as the following quotation will show.

Newburgh Hamilton, whose career hitherto had been concerned with farce (*The Petticoat-Plotter*, 1712) and comedy (*The Doating Lovers*, 1715), assisted Handel in the preparation of *Alexander's Feast* in 1735. What he has to say in his preface to that Ode is interesting and instructive. His modesty commends the man as also does his musical perception and his loyalty to Handel.

. . . I was determined not to take any unwarrantable liberty with that poem, which has so long done honour to the nation, and which no man can add to or abridge in anything material, without injuring it. I therefore confined myself to a plain division of it into airs, recitatives or choruses, looking upon the words in general so sacred as scarcely to violate one in the order of its first place. How I have succeeded, the world is to judge; and whether I have preserved that beautiful description of the passions so exquisitely drawn, at the same time I strove to reduce them to the present taste in sounds. I confess my principal view was not to lose this favourable opportunity of its being set to musick by that great master, who has with pleasure undertaken the task, and who only is capable of doing it justice; whose compositions have long shown that they can conquer even the most obstinate partiality, and inspire life into the most senseless words.

If this entertainment can, in the least degree, give satisfaction to the real judges of poetry or musick, I shall think myself happy in having promoted it, being persuaded that it is next to an improbability to offer the world anything in those arts more perfect than the united labours and utmost efforts of a Dryden and a Handel.

Five or six years later Hamilton went one better—a combination of Milton and Handel and this is from his preface to the wordbook of *Samson*.

That poem, indeed, never was divided by Milton into acts or scenes, nor designed (as he hints in his preface) for the stage; but given only as the plan of a tragedy with choruses, after the manner of the ancients. But as Mr Handel had so happily introduced here oratorios, a musical drama, whose subjects must be scriptural, and in which the solemnity of church musick is agreeably united with the most pleasing airs of the stage, it would have been an irretrievable loss to have neglected the opportunity of that great master's doing justice to this work; he having already added new life and spirit to some of the finest things in the English language, particularly that inimitable Ode of Dryden's, which no age nor nation ever excelled.

As we have so great a genius amongst us, it is a pity that so many mean artifices have been lately used to blast all his endeavours, and in him ruin the art itself; but he has the satisfaction of being encouraged by all true lovers and real judges of musick; in a more especial manner by that illustrious person [Frederick, Prince of Wales], whose high rank only serves to make his knowledge in all arts and sciences as conspicuous as his power and inclination to patronize them.

Samson Agonistes possessed from the musician's point of view, as Newburgh Hamilton noticed, the most commendable attributes. It was a drama, but contrived for reading rather than for stage performance; it was divided between principals and chorus; it was nominally 'sacred' in origin; and it was not unfamiliar. It had been, as Dr Johnson puts it, 'too much admired . . . and it is only by a blind confidence in the reputation of Milton, that a drama can be praised in which the intermediate parts have neither cause nor consequence, neither hasten nor retard the catastrophe'. It is to be regretted that Johnson was not musician enough to detect that manner in which Handel made the dramatic potentialities actual.

Now Handel, who probably was not unaware of the main stream of eighteenth century Milton criticism from Addison to Johnson nor of the absorption of Miltonic mannerisms by writers as varied as Pope, Akenside, and Dyer, would have discovered in *Samson Agonistes* much of personal relevance, First from the standpoint of religion, in respect of which we may quote Professor Denis Saurat. '*Samson Agonistes* is a return to simplicity. Milton gives up the complications of dogma, fall, and restoration, and frankly sets his drama in Samson's soul—a drama which is led towards precise aims by Destiny, by God. God is more mysterious and more dreadful; He is no longer the all too clear logician of *Paradise Lost*; He is the incomprehensible and yet just Power that presides over the course of the World. . . . In *Samson* he [Milton] takes the next step and frees himself from dogma; all he keeps of it is God-Destiny.' The God-Destiny motive is the metaphysical juncture between Handel and Milton.

Then there is the matter of humanity. Handel, both by training and instinct, contrived all his art from a human (or humane) viewpoint, so that within his drama might be represented each individual member of his audience—and himself also. What Addison says of *Paradise Lost* is applicable to *Samson* and ultimately to Handel as well as to Milton. 'Milton's poem is admirable in this respect, since it is impossible for any of its readers, whatever nation, country, or people he may belong to, not to be related to the persons who are the principal actors in it; but what is still infinitely more to its advantage, the principal actors in this poem are not only our progenitors, but our representatives. We have an actual interest in everything they do, and no less than our interest happiness is concerned, and lies at stake in their behaviour.' Had he not possessed something of the visionary's powers Handel would never have made a great work of art out of Milton's poem. Had he shared Johnson's viewpoint he would never have set the subject, all of which goes to show that either Handel was not entirely of the eighteenth century or the eighteenth century was different from our general conception of it. Both of these statements are, in fact, true.

The matter of textual edition calls for comment. Milton has 1758 lines in his poem. Handel can only use as much as can be compressed into less than 400 lines. Newburgh Hamilton is to be congratulated (a little belatedly) on his skill with scissors and paste. It is out of place to cavil when,

in the name of broadcasting, similar or more drastic ampu-
tations are made in literary programmes. No doubt Handel
would willingly have set to music the whole of *Samson
Agonistes* magnificently, but there are limits to the powers
of public endurance—as Wagner and Shaw later discovered.
Besides, a little Milton can carry much music. What the
poet defines in detailed verbal ramification the musician can
illustrate by other means. Hence the frequent paradox of
mediocre verse provoking sublimity in music. In the case
of *Samson*, however, the Miltonic key phrases illuminate the
mind by their own splendour and by their own associations
while the music moves with equal majesty to its preordained
end. For instance, the brilliance of the two concluding items
summarizes musically (and adequately) the content of *At a
Solemn Musick*—the cherubic host might operate less am-
biguously were they not compelled by Hamilton to essay
new branches of percussion with golden wires. We know—
or should know—what Milton wrote and once the clue
is given we have no further need of words. Parenthetically
it may be suggested that Parry fails, not ingloriously, to
resolve Milton into music by writing Miltonically whereas
Handel throws the radiance of Handel at selected points in
the Miltonic heavens. A case in point is the most poignant
passage in the whole of *Samson*—if not indeed in the whole
of Handel—'Total eclipse'. This air—or is it not more
truthfully a recitative?—carries within it the spirit of 100
lines of verse and it is difficult to believe that anything said
by Milton is omitted. Handel adds the tremendous effect of
melodic climax (that at the fourth bar of the vocal part with
its musical anticipation of the verbal climax gives a sense of
burning pain to the agony of Samson's darkness), of rests,
of melismata. So unsparing is Milton in delineation of mental
and physical affliction that the chorus asks—

> *Can this be hee,*
> *That Heroic, that Renown'd*
> *Irresistible* Samson?

With Handel there is no need of such question. The heroic parts of Samson are never submerged.

This oratorio has maintained much of its early popularity (it was much more admired in 1743 than *Messiah*) partly because of its sentimental appeal—Beard's singing of 'Total Eclipse' in the last years of Handel's life, the composer being then himself blind, used to bring tears to the eyes of audiences—and partly on account of its choruses. To say that Handel achieved in *Samson* a certainty in his handling of the choral unit would be to suggest, improperly, that the early oratorios, not to mention the ecclesiastical music proper and, in part, the operas were in this respect undistinguished. What was added, however, in *Samson* was a sense of homogeneity. The final chorus of *Esther* was too magnific, the double choirs of *Deborah* were unpliable, *Saul* on occasion pursued a pedestrian course, while *Israel in Egypt* was overbalanced by its torrents of homophony. *Samson* has strength and also elegance. It looks forward to the late eighteenth century in manner whereas its predecessors echo many times habits of the seventeenth century. The choruses are by turns dramatic, picturesque, imploratory, and reflective. For brilliance in natural definition 'O first created beam', with its sequential repetitions leading to a wide harmonic spread in C major—Haydn's key for the same project—and 'With thunder armed' are tremendous. There is in these choruses a sense of philosophic reflection and not merely the fascination of Handel's palette. In the realm of high spirits, whether of secular or sacred prompting, there are the choruses of the priests of Dagon and the contrasting choruses, instinct with an almost rational confidence, of the Israelites.

The opening chorus of the priests of Dagon (the dynamic energy of the unaccompanied octaves might be regarded as a devastating Handelian forehand drive) forecasts that magnificent passage of festival reporting which Milton commences—

Occasions drew me early to this City,
And as the gates I enter'd with Sun-rise,
The morning Trumpets Festival proclaim'd
Through each high street: . . .

We ourselves are part of the scene whether in the company
of Handel or Milton, or both. And as part of this scene
should be construed the overture.

On the side of tragedy *Samson* gives to the chorus 'To
dust his glory they would tread' which overtakes Micah's
'Return, O God of hosts' and in so doing impresses forcibly
the urgency of the plea. Then there is the brief sublimity of
'Weep, Israel, weep'. The choral surround to this drama
makes *mise en scène* superfluous. Just as *Samson Agonistes* is
unstageable so is *Samson*.

Streatfield neatly, and apparently unconsciously, ties up
the Handel and Milton moral interpretation of the plot:
'the disgust with which he [Handel] regarded the sensuality
that he saw rampant round him is, I think, to be read in
Samson by those that have eyes to see. I have already pointed
out how fond Handel was of fixing on a word or a phrase
and making it the text on which to ground a discourse. In
"Then round about the starry throne" he seizes upon the
words, "from all this earthly grossness quit", and turning
as it were with loathing from the sordid and sensual amours
of Samson and Delilah, he lifts his voice in a triumphant
paean in praise of chastity'. By the side of this we may set
Professor Saurat's masterly handling of Milton's thesis on
sensuality the conqueror of reason. The secret of Handel's
own life remains still secret but his place in that section of
society least prone to wantonness is a possible guarantee of
his private point of view on morals and morality. By 1742,
in any case, he had arrived at an age when, in general,
those energetically and happily employed in their chosen
profession manage to subdue passion to reason.

But Handel was more human than Milton. His moral

standpoint is less obvious. He presents his characters as he sees them, tempers their failings with charity, and leaves us to exercise our own judgement. The Samson of *Samson* is less classically heroic than the original of *Samson Agonistes* just as Saul is more humanly shaped than Lear. The standards of common humanity always form Handel's touchstone of criticism. The blindness of Samson, the bewildered, impotent rage of 'Why does the God of Israel sleep', the despiteful rejection of Delilah bring the drama into easy perspective. These are expositions of emotion common and unproblematic. Handel's mode of presentation is inspired with genius not in sudden, sharp intuitive bursts but in the climactic sense which enables him to put each aria and recitative in significant relationship one to another. The course of Samson's decline is enriched by Handel by the introduction of an inspired lyrical scene from the *Ode on the Morning of Christ's Nativity*. This interpolation is only due to a brilliant appreciation of dramatic propriety and a close acquaintance with Milton. What was Handel's part in suggesting 'Thus when the sun'? We do not know. We can only feel that the incisive pointing of this—almost the loveliest of all his lyrical conceptions—enhances once again the human qualities of the hero. The preceding recitative takes the former dynamism of the fallen leader and reminds of what was. We are taken before the throne of Jehovah. And then God and man merge in the iridescence of sunset. Samson passes from sight, singing his own threnode. 'Total eclipse' ushered in the inspissation of physical darkness: 'Thus when the sun' points the compass towards light and repose and to a spiritual state of tranquillity. Samson joins Saul as his obsequies are served by the same funeral march (there is an alternative, but, in comparison inapt).

The weakness of *Saul* lay in the disproportion of the characterization. *Samson* can provoke no such observation. Micah, Manoah, Harapha and Dalila are accurate and carefully contrived individuals of memorable significance. Micah is, historically, mythical but he is a convenience for the introduction of alto solos. His observations are drawn from among those of Milton's chorus and he may, therefore, be taken as the choragus. This is clearly indicated in the coalescence of solo and chorus in 'Return, O Lord of hosts' and also in 'The holy one of Israel'.

Manoah reveals that favourite figure in Handel's catalogue of virtue. Age, dignity, affection, and pride blend in that same autumnal russet as enfolds Abinoam in *Deborah*. Harapha similarly is a type. Handel had conventions for his giants, braggarts, and Philistines—metaphorically speaking—from Polyphemus to Hercules. In these characters it is not wickedness that is pilloried so much as ignorance and obtuseness: the villains are even attractive and companionable—victims of the doctrine of original sin by some mischance unredeemed and dangerous to society only because they have learned no constructive purpose in life. Samson figures the artist, the poet, the maker: Harapha the stupid and insensitive sceptic. Handel refuses to have 'his giantship somewhat crestfall'n' or to diminish his 'unconscionable strides'; he labels Harapha with the exuberance of 'Honour and arms', the proud flamboyance of 'Presuming slave', the cheap and easy mockery of the duet 'Presume not on thy God'—and we see before us a 'tongue-doubtie' rascal with a childish faith in the thesis that might is right. It is impossible to believe that Handel was treating the type in the abstract. He portrayed his associates—and ours. His Harapha is as alive, as true, and as relevant as Smollett's Commodore Trunnion or Captain Oakum.

So too Dalila is something of a Becky Sharp. Handel wastes no time in characterizing this attractive, spirited, heartless wanton, and Saint-Saëns, who complained of Handel's prolixity, might have noted with advantage this masterpiece of brevity. In the avian aria 'With plaintive notes' Dalila slyly exhibits her blatant charms: then, the

I

sensuous charms having been supposed to conquer Samson's despite, she proclaims with more directness her faith and truth. This is supported by the chorus of attendant virgins, whose duet with their mistress harks back in its final tirade of consecutive thirds to the days and practice of Steffani. But Samson merely allows charm to arouse his bitter memories and we are plunged into the anger, recrimination, and vigour of the duet 'Traitor (traitress) to love'. It will be noticed that Samson has the last word, that 'the thorn intestin' retires, defeated, while the chorus summon their energy for the moral observation (Handel was here proud in bachelordom)

> *Therefore God's universal Law*
> *Gave to the man despotic power*
> *Over his female in due awe . . .*

emended by Hamilton to (and here we discern a difference of domestic outlook between the seventeenth and the eighteenth centuries)

> *To man God's universal law*
> *Gave power to keep his wife in awe . . .*

To isolate further choruses or arias would be to encourage the fallacy that such may be lifted from their respective contexts and presented as concert 'items'. At the same time it would be impossible to omit mention of the great focal chorus 'Fix'd in his everlasting seat', for this symbolizes the intellectual problem: Jehovah or Dagon? This climax occurs—the solution lies in futurity—at the end of the second part of the oratorio. For a moment Handel takes his mind away from the abstract problem and allows his eyes to follow Milton's imagination to where

> *The Stars, with deep amaze,*
> *Stand fixt in steadfast gaze.*

Hamilton (quite unnecessarily) alters the actual words, but Handel, with the whole sense of the *Ode on the Morning of Christ's Nativity* behind him replaces the poetic aspiration in one of the simplest and greatest passages in the whole heritage of music. Then there is the elegiac solo *cum* chorus 'Glorious hero' which, moving between D minor and G minor, foreshadows the 'requiem æternam' spirituality of Mozart and recalls the funereal rose-petals of *Dido and Aeneas*.

The first singers of *Samson* were famed for gifts other than their *bel canto*—with the exception of Signora Avolio. They were Mrs Clive, Mrs Cibber, Mr Beard, and Mr Savage. They will be discussed in more detail at a later point. Here let it be recorded that few singers at that time existed possessing the devotion to Handel and the intellectual capacity to pierce the surface of the music other than those within the circle of his intimacy.

On February 24, 1743, Horace Walpole wrote—with the first performance of *Samson* fresh in mind—'Handel has set up an oratorio against the Opera, and succeeds. He has hired all the goddesses from the farces, and the singers of roast-beef from between the acts at both theatres, with a man with one note in his voice [Beard] and a girl without ever an one [Mrs Cibber], and so they sing and make brave hallelujahs, and the good company *encore* the recitative, if it happens to have any cadence like what they call a tune.' That was one reaction—that of the sophisticated man of the world. But against the hedonism—we have already referred to the polarity of the later Handel oratorio—of Walpole was the high-mindedness of Catherine Talbot, the adopted daughter of the Archbishop of Canterbury: 'I really cannot help thinking this kind of entertainment must necessarily have some effect in correcting the levity of the age; and let an audience be ever so thoughtless, they can scarcely come away, I should think, without being the better for an evening so spent.'

In 1743 England was on the edge of revolution: a year earlier John Wesley had been denied access to the pulpit at Epworth.

The Messiah Bicentenary, 1742-1942

ST. PATRICK'S CATHEDRAL, DUBLIN
Monday, 13th April, 1942, at 8 p.m.

CHRIST CHURCH CATHEDRAL, DUBLIN
Tuesday, 14th April, 1942, at 8 p.m.

THE UNITED CATHEDRAL CHOIRS

GEORGE FREDERICK HANDEL was born at Halle in Saxony in 1685, the year in which Bach was born. He came to England in 1711 and made his home there for the rest of his life. He was in Dublin for nine months from November, 1741. Here he met with worthy appreciation On Easter Tuesday, 13th April, 1742, his greatest Oratorio, *Messiah*, was sung for the first time. It was performed in the Music Hall in in Fishamble Street, close to Christ Church Cathedral. Handel conducted, and was assisted by the Choirs of both Dublin Cathedrals Handel's last public appearance was at a performance of this Oratorio Eight days later he died, on the anniversary of its first performance aged 74. He was buried in Westminster Abbey. He left behind him a name and popularity which have not been rivalled by any other master musician.

St. Patrick's Cathedral		Christ Church Cathedral	
GENTLEMEN OF THE CHOIR, 1742		GENTLEMEN OF THE CHOIR, 1742	
Mr. Worrall	Mr. Jones	Mr. Worrall	Mr. Smith
Mr. Church	Mr. Phibbs	Mr. Taylor	Mr. Mason
Mr. Bailey	Mr. Tavernor	Mr. Jones	Mr. Church
Mr. Hall	Mr. Woffington	Mr. Phipps	Mr. Ward
Mr. Lambe	Mr. Smith	Mr. Bailey	Mr. Carter
Mr. Ward	Mr. Hill	Mr. Lambe	Mr. Hill
Mr. Colgan		Mr. Rosingrave, *Organist,*	
Mr. Rosingrave, *Organist,*		and 8 Choristers	
and 8 Choristers.			

JONATHAN SWIFT,
DEAN OF ST PATRICK'S

CHARLES COBBE,
DEAN OF CHRIST CHURCH

GENTLEMEN OF THE CHOIR, 1942		GENTLEMEN OF THE CHOIR, 1942	
Mr. Hall	Mr. Gill	Mr Horan	Mr. Whitehead
Mr. Grace	Mr. Marchant	Mr. Watson	Mr. Selfe
Mr. Martin	Mr. Thompson	Mr Rafter	Mr. Cowle
Mr. Watson	Mr. Scott	Mr Maddison	Mr. Winter
Mr. Walsh	Mr. E. G. Reeves	Mr. McCullough	Mr. Flood
Mr. Dawson	Mr. Mason	Mr. Begley	Mr. Midgley
Mr. Harte	Mr E C Reeves	Mr Weaving, *Organist,*	
Mr. Godfrey		and 20 Choristers.	
Dr. Hewson, *Organist,*			
and 24 Choristers			

DAVID F. R. WILSON,
DEAN OF ST. PATRICK'S

E. H. LEWIS-CROSBY,
DEAN OF CHRIST CHURCH

Title-page of the Bicentenary Messiah, Dublin 1942; with the names of the choristers in the first performance

Chapter Eight

JOSEPH AND BELSHAZZAR

BY 1743 Handel may be said to have made the composition of oratorios, as previously of operas, a habit. A new oratorio was an annual event. After *Samson* came *Semele* which, not being an oratorio at all but an English opera without action, falls outside our terms of reference. After *Semele*, *Joseph* was offered as a token of proper piety. Here, almost for the first time, we must confess a lack of inspiration. The judicious taste of the time appears to have found itself in agreement with posterity—a rare accident—and we may have doubts as to whether Handel himself (always a good and objective critic of his own music) was very enthusiastic. He started to complain of his singers and when he did this it was sometimes in self-defence. 'Handel', says Mrs Delany referring to the rehearsals, 'was mightily out of humour about it, for Sullivan, who is to sing Joseph, is a *block* with a very fine voice, and Beard has *no voice at all* [this smells of collusion with Walpole]. The part which Francescina is to have (Joseph's wife) will not admit of much variety, but I hope it will be well received.'

Handel's dullest work appears indirectly to reflect the torpor of the times. The resilience of the wits of Queen Anne's day was past and the last vestiges of Restoration influence had passed from artistic life. The refusal to permit Wesley to preach at Epworth and the publication of the

hymns (1740-2) were symptomatic, but Wesley's genius had
not yet crossed with the evangelistic talent of Whitefield to
stir the popular heart to that zeal for self-expression in pity,
hope, love and fear which was to support on crested waves
the finer effulgence of literary romanticism. In 1743
Richardson with *Pamela*, published in 1740, to his credit,
Fielding with an ephemeral list of burlesque and from-the-
French dramas and melodramas, Smollett, distressed by
metropolitan lack of appreciation, and Sterne, as yet quite
unknown, had shown little to suggest that in them reposed
the supremacy of the English novel. In 1743 poetry moved
in gentle waters, steered by Thomson—perhaps Handel
knew him through the intermediacy of Quin, Gray (something of an authority on the side of musical research),
Young, Collins, Akenside, and Shenstone (another devotee
of Handel). The age of Johnson began inauspiciously with
uninspiring work on parliamentary reports—records
frequently of what ought to have been said rather than what
was said—for Edward Cave. 1743 was an urbane, dull and
complacent point of repose—the one year which may be
selected to satisfy the conventional estimate of the whole
century. Even Trevelyan spreads characteristics which we
might properly find at selected points only (or, possibly,
in combination in the mid-forties) over a period of forty
years.

It is only in the years that followed (1740-80) that we find a generation of men wholly characteristic of the Eighteenth Century ethos,
a society with a mental outlook of its own, self-poised, self-judged,
and self-approved, freed from the disturbing passions of the past,
and not yet troubled by the anxieties about a very different future
which was soon to be brought upon the scene by the Industrial and
French Revolutions.

The war by 1743 failed to stimulate either hate or pity and
as for the victory of Dettingen—unearned and unexpected—
not even Handel's *Te Deum* could convince a nation inured
o military impotence since the great days of Marlborough

of its significance. It took the Young Pretender to excite the dormant virilities. But that was in 1745.

James Miller (1706-1744) was by no means the least notable dramatist in a period whose insignificance can be gauged from the complete oblivion into which he was so soon to fall. And yet, as the record of a brief career unfolds, respect gathers round one whose versatility was not untypical. Miller was a Wadham man, a dramatist with satirical inclinations in his undergraduate days, who took holy orders. The eighteenth century parson was rarely negative. He did something to justify, from the economist's point of view, his existence—indeed necessity often forced extra-pastoral activity—even if in surprising channels. Miller, who—in 1743 in fact—returned to the vicarage, over which his father had been master before him, in Upcerne, Dorset-shire, combined two separate careers with something of the verve, if less of the success, of Trollope. As with Trollope, official life had its worries. Ecclesiastical preferment was denied to him because on the one hand he was a high churchman and on the other a writer of plays. His superiors disapproved on both counts. In 1737 he had made enemies among the Templars in his caricature, in *The Coffee House*, of their favourite recreation room at Mother Yarrow's. In the first part of his dramatic career we distinguish in Miller broad interests and a pen competent to annoy. Which at least means that he was not negligible. After *The Humours of Oxford* (which reached the boards of Drury Lane in 1730) came, in 1732, the inevitable ballad opera *Vanelia*. Then *The Man of Taste* after Molière.

At this point, the year being 1735, we discover in Miller a tendency towards reform. *The Man of Taste* is set up as antidote to vice. In an earlier play, (*The Mother-in-Law; or The Doctor the Disease*) also from Molière whose works were translated by the industrious Miller and H. Baker, it was claimed that the play contained 'not . . . one indecent Expression, not one immoral Thought'. *The Universal*

Passion (1737) extends the prophylactic policy: 'a strict
Regard' is paid 'to Decency and good Manners' because
'People may be very well diverted with Exhibitions of this
kind without the least Violation being offered to Virtue,
Truth or Humanity, and that the world is at present happily
inclin'd to support what is produced with that Intention'.

The very man, it might be thought, for the preparation of
a libretto for an oratorio destined to whet the new moralistic appetite. Miller was also a fervent Handelian. This he
discloses in the customary preamble—addressed to the Duke
of Montague—attached to his part of *Joseph and His
Brethren*.

> May it please your Grace, I have no other apology to make for
> presuming to lay the following performance at your Grace's feet,
> than the countenance you are pleased to give to the refined and
> sublime entertainments of this kind, and the generous patronage
> you manifest towards the great master, by whose divine harmony they
> are supported. A master meritorious of such a patron, as he may be
> said, without the least adulation, to have shown a higher degree of
> excellence in each of the various kinds of composition, than any one
> who has preceded him ever arrived at in a single branch of it; and to
> have so peculiar a felicity in always making his strain the tongue
> of his subject, that this music is sure to talk to the purpose, whether
> the words it is set to do so or not. [An arrow which finds its mark.]
> 'Tis a pity, however, my Lord, that such a genius should be put
> to the drudgery of hammering for fire where there is no flint, and
> of giving a sentiment to the poet's metre before he can give one to
> his own melody.

And so on, until Miller generously and truthfully admits the
poverty of his own invention.

The difficulty with *Joseph* is that it is firmly wedged between the stools of sanctity and secularity. *Semele* is a glorious work, free, rich, voluptuous. The qualities which made
Semele were now recognizably not those appropriate to
'sacred' oratorio. In 1744 the net is beginning to tighten.
Handel is three years distant from his last opera, maturity and
ill-health and the cabals of the faithless as well as the zeal of
the faithful have caused him to alter course, Miller has

defined the new 'entertainment' in terms of refinement and sublimity. In brief an evangelistic wind is getting up: the Victorian approach to Handel is in anticipation.

Mrs Delany, now married to the Dean of Down and half conscious of the responsibilities of her new dignity, writes:

> Semele is charming; the more I hear it the better I like it, and as I am a subscriber I shall not fail one night. But it being a profane [a hard adjective would never have come from Mrs Pendarves] story D.D. [the Dean] does not think it proper for him to go; but when Joseph and Samson is performed I shall persuade him to go—you know how much he delights in music. They say Samson is to be next Friday, for Semele has a strong party against it, viz. the fine ladies, petit maîtres, and *ignoramus's*. All the opera people are enraged at Handel, but Lady Cobham, Lady Westmoreland, and Lady Chesterfield [a pupil of Handel at one time] never fail it.

There a contemporary reporter epitomizes the musico-political situation.

In the story of Joseph there are two points of high drama which, at almost any other time in his career, Handel would have lifted to climactic intensity. The one is the interpretation of Pharaoh's dream, the exposition of which scene compares unfavourably with the necromantic passages in *Saul, Hercules, Amadigi* or *Belshazzar;* the other the recognition scene.

In comparison with the story in Genesis (xlv. 1 *et seq.*) it will be seen that Miller's verbal extravagance—a fault peculiar to most librettists ancient and modern—has lost the day.

Miller was a sentimentalist and traces of the growing country-life influence in contemporary verse are allowed entrance to the text. When Miller appears to qualify as a candidate for admission to the ranks of the Wessex school (one would expect poets to grow on every tree in Upcerne) Handel falls into the felicitous ways of *L'Allegro* and anticipates the wayside sketches of *Susanna*. In *Athaliah* the *bizarrerie* of the music helped to suggest a unity of place. In *Joseph* the classical concepts of the unities go by the board.

Time marches on alarmingly so that within half an hour of her marriage Asenath is contemplating the fruits of her union. At one moment we are by the banks of Nile, the next we are ruminating more temperately under the influence of English landscape. Thus the drama itself falls into second place and what we recollect from the oratorio are episodes: the ode to Autumn by Phanor, the exaltation by Joseph of the pleasures of the rustic life, the fluminal rhapsody of Asenath. These are occasions of charm to be set by the side of the quiet fluency and affectionate precision of Dyer or Shenstone or Matthew Green, poets whom Handel may well have read. Dyer's *Grongar Hill* is under the spell, and Handel himself was from time to time, of *L'Allegro* and *Il Penseroso*. At this point, and in case the reader grows sceptical of literary influence on the music of Handel, we may refer to W. L. Renwick. 'In the eighteenth century, painting and music were living arts which exerted their power upon poetry as poetry did upon them. The arts did not live in isolation from one another or from social life, as they did in the nineteenth century, when literature enjoyed an unwholesome predominance, and when that balance and integration of the arts, learning, and society which we call a civilization broke down under the combined impact of romanticism and industrialism.'

By Green's vignettes in 'The Spleen' may be placed the graceful, careful simplicity of

31.

It is not the assumption of folk-song mannerism which allows to music topographical assurance: it is the capacity for transmuting the fine essence of contemporary vision into terms of music. There is in *Orlando*, in *Ricardo I*, *Acis and Galatea* and *Serse* broad, realistic expression of scenic symbolism—the art of Wagner, of the practised narrative hand. *L'Allegro*, *Susanna*, parts of *Solomon*, of *Semele* and of *Joseph* show less of the elementary tradition of scene-shifting in exhibiting the particularism of the mid-eighteenth century pastoral tradition.

The cool fragrance of the pastoral interpolations is all that *Joseph* may hope to be remembered by. For the rest we are too long aware of Handel's penchant for prolixity, while the choruses are of George Eliot's 'mechanical-dramatic'. The flamboyance of Pharaoh's 'Since the Race of Time, began', and the cakes and ale revelry of the chorus in the succeeding epithalamium may be excepted from the general stricture, although here again invidious comparisons can be made with the glitter of *Athaliah* and the debauchery of *Belshazzar*. The overture, sombrely clad in E minor, and with a fine fugal essay in the middle movement, and the concluding Hallelujah, amply emphasized by three trumpets, revert to the mood of correlative movements in *Messiah*.

Harriet Byron, in *Sir Charles Grandison* produced an excellent homily on the subject of Handelian appreciation.

'As you know', she said to Sir Charles, 'that great part of the beauty of this performance arises from the proper transitions from one different strain to another, any one song must lose greatly by being taken out of its place; and I fear—'

'Fear nothing, Miss Byron,' interrupted Sir Charles, 'your obligingness, as well as your observation, entitle you to all allowances.'

Belshazzar is one of the most clear examples of Miss Byron's thesis: a completely unified artistic entity. The theme has such topicality that wonderment can only be expressed at its almost total neglect. The same sentiment was issued more than seventy years ago, by Macfarren.

The letters extant from Handel to Jennens demonstrate Handel's excitement at the opportunities afforded him in the libretto which, incidentally, is quite one of the best with which he ever had to deal.

On June 9, 1744, we find Handel acknowledging receipt of the first act. Actual composition did not, as the customary inscription on the manuscript (Angefangen den 23 Agost 1744) shows, start till later. But ideas were germinating. Handel and Jennens worked in fairly complete accord. At all times there is between artistic collaborators a pull of conflicting *amours-propres* but Handel (no longer let the myth of the hardened old egoist persist) was willing to listen to a rational argument from his colleague. On July 19—he had apparently been in the country on holiday—he wrote as follows:

> At my arrival in London, which was Yesterday, I immediately perused the Act of the Oratorio with which you favor'd me, and, the little time only I had it, gives me great Pleasure. Your reasons for the Length of the first Act are intirely satisfactory to me, and it is likewise my opinion to have the following Acts short. I shall be very glad, and much obliged to you, if you will soon favour me with the remaining Acts. Be pleased to point out those passages in the *Messiah* which you think require altering. . . .

Jennens spread himself over the first act to lay out thoroughly the *dramatis personae*, the military reconnaissances of Cyrus and the portending moral issues. Act II effectively brings military operations to the stage of activity while Belshazzar carouses, 'his wives, concubines and lords, drinking out of the Jewish temple-vessels, and singing the praises of their gods'. The dramatic peak of this section is the interpretation by Daniel of the writing on the wall. The third act is climactic with the slaughter of Belshazzar, the rout of his undisciplined hosts, the act of submission by Nicotris, and the conventional attribution of victory over world, flesh, and devil to God.

The quality of Jennens at his best is exemplified by the passage with which Nicotris—whose second sight and intuition rank her again with Calphurnia—opens. A diatribe from the eighteenth century against imperialism sounds oddly in the ear but here, nevertheless, it is.

> *Vain, fluctuating state of human empire!*
> *First, small and weak, it scarcely rears its head,*
> *Scarce stretching out its helpless infant arms,*
> *Implores protection of its neighbour states,*
> *Who nurse it to their hurt. Anon it strives*
> *For power and wealth, and spurns at opposition.*
> *Arrived to full maturity, it grasps*
> *At all within its reach, o'erleaps all bounds,*
> *Robs, ravages, and wastes the frighted world.*

At length grown old, and swell'd to bulk enormous,
The monster in its proper bowels feeds
Pride, luxury, corruption, perfidy,
That prey upon her vitals. Of her weakness
Some other rising power advantage takes,
(Unequal match!) plies with repeated strokes
Her infirm, aged trunk: she nods—she totters—
She falls—alas, never to rise again.
The victor state, upon her ruins
Runs the same shadowy round of fancied greatness,
Meets the same certain end. . . .

In this passage, which in the truest sense of the word is classic, Handel meets Jennen's sublimity of objective and judicial utterance. This particular recitative of Nicotris is among the most nervous and tense dramatic essays ever written by Handel. But this is to anticipate; on August 21 the second act had been delivered, at which point Handel commenced the composition of the oratorio.

Part I terminated with this note: *Septembr* 3, 1744, *fine della parte prima den* 5 *Septembr völlig geendiget.* On September 13, the second part finished three days earlier, Handel wrote again to Jennens with rising enthusiasm.

> Your most excellent Oratorio has given me great delight in setting it to Musick, and still engages me warmly. It is indeed a Noble Piece, very grand and uncommon; [How much Handel was of his age is evidenced by his literary style. 'Grand and uncommon' is almost the ultimate of appreciative comment on the side of the picturesque and romantic.] it has furnished me with expressions [opportunities of being expressive or emotional], and has given me Opportunity to some very particular Ideas, besides so many great Chorus [sic] I entreat you heartily to favour me soon with the last Act, which I expect with anxiety, that I may regulate myself the better to the length of it. . . .

Within three weeks the last act arrived and Handel, always with an eye on the limitation of performance acknowledged it thus:

London, October 2, 1744

Dear Sir,

I received the 3rd Act with a great deal of pleasure, as you can imagine and you may believe that I think it a very sublime Oratorio, only it really is too long; if I should extend the Musick, it would last four hours and more. I retrench'd already a great deal of the Musick, that I might preserve the poetry as much as I could; yet it still may be shortened. The anthems come in very properly; but would not the words, 'Tell it out among the Heathen that the Lord is King', be sufficient for our Chorus. The Anthem, 'I will magnify Thee, O God, my King, and I will praise Thy Name for ever and ever', Vers. 'The Lord preserveth all them that love him; but scattereth the ungodly', Vers. and Chorus. 'My Mouth shall speak the praise of the Lord, and let all flesh give thanks unto his holy name for ever and ever. Amen'; concludes well the Oratorio.

Yours, etc.
George Frideric Handel.

The two Chandos anthems, impressed on the suggestion of Jennens, who would thus appear to have been well acquainted with the Handel canon, were remodelled for *Belshazzar*. The refurbishing of old and nearly forgotten works was a constant practice of Handel (and indeed of Bach), who hated to see good music lying idle. It is a practice only possible in a period in which music has a good deal of utilitarian significance. And it is this mark of utilitarianism which we might accept as the principal characteristic of eighteenth century music.

Belshazzar was put on at Covent Garden on March 27, 1745 and was repeated two days later and also on April 23, on which night the season ('which' says Burney, 'he began November 3rd., and continued to his great loss, and the nation's disgrace, till the 23rd. April') closed. It has generally been stated that in this year Handel was bankrupt. In fact he wasn't. However, he was far from well, as Lady Harris wrote to her cousin James Harris, and fashionable society was proving as inconstant in loyalty as fashionable society always does. Smollett, in discontent, penury and in a strange and inhospitable land, noticed the situation in his polemic *Advice*.

> *Again shall Handel raise his laurelled brow,*
> *Again shall harmony with rapture glow!*
> *The spells dissolve, the combination breaks,*
> *And rival Punch no more in terror squeaks.*
> *Lo, Russel falls a sacrifice to whim*
> *And starts amazed in Newgate from his dream,*
> *With trembling hands implores their promised aid*
> *And sees their favour like a vision fade.*

Nevertheless there were the faithful. Catherine Talbot applauded the oratorio, clearly on account of its dramatic propensities.

Unfashionable that I am, I was, I own, highly delighted the other night at his [Handel's] last oratorio. 'Tis called Belshazzar, the story of the taking of Babylon by Cyrus; and the music, in spite of all that very bad performers could do to spoil it, equal to anything I ever heard. There is a chorus of Babylonians deriding Cyrus from their walls, that has the best expression of scornful laughter imaginable. Another of the Jews, where the name Jehovah is introduced first with a moment's silence and then with a full swell of music, so solemn that I think it is the most striking lesson against common genteel swearing I ever met with.

One may disregard Miss Talbot when she steps into the company of Jane Austen, *in re* 'common genteel swearing', but like a good critic she substantiates her opinions with evidence to which we may turn.

The first chorus to which she refers, 'Behold, by Persia's Hero made', strikes initially by percussive reiteration, to which in martial ardour we may compare the welcome-home chorus of *Hercules* and the epinicion of *Saul;* then the city moat, the Euphrates, (we build even anti-tank ditches in vain) is depicted thus dimensionally:

32.

How broad   the   ditch,   how deep   it   falls

next an echo passage borrowed in essence from Purcell:
then a series of sober revelations in madrigalian fugato:

33.

Twenty times the sun Round the great year his   course   shall run;

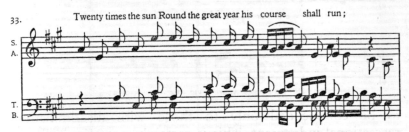

a brilliant essay in auto-suggestion: finally a heavy finale
based on this waggish subject with upturned tail.

34.

Thy wise at - tempt   will find us   sport,

Nor should we overlook the neatness of the technique
which brings back the instrumental introduction in absolute
conclusion.

The second chorus to call forth Miss Talbot's approbation
was the clamant 'Sing, O ye Heav'ns', a movement—or
rather two movements, prelude and fugue—which need not
detain us. Here is the orthodox mastery of the quick-witted
dramatist eyeing easy effectiveness. The mood is of the
opening pages of *Saul*, but less thrilling. The faithful excited
Handel less than the infidel. Thus Persians and Babylonians
come off with fresher music than the Jews. 'See from his
post Euphrates flies' is a powerful essay in realism, based on

K

the fluctuating river motive, also to be found in *L'Allegro*, albeit in different circumstances. The middle section, antiphonally divided between high and low voices, is an elegy. At the end the music moralizes fugally.

While this chorus is an unsatisfactory artistic experience (the fugue is the trouble) the ripe ribaldry of the Nobles' 'Ye tutelar Gods' is magnificent. This is a toper's song:

35.

Ye tut - e - lar gods of our em - pire look down And

see what rich tro - phies your vic - tor - y crown; ⸺

to be commended only to those with discriminating recreational judgement. This is certainly not Miss Talbot's cup of tea. Here the music of the oratorio reaches its crux. What the nobility express is continued in the debauchery of Belshazzar's 'Let the deep bowl'. And then, as the king taunts Jehovah, 'as he is speaking, a hand appears writing on the wall over against him; he sees it, turns pale with fear, drops the bowl of wine, falls back in his seat trembling from head to foot, and his knees knocking against each other'. Then let the music speak for itself:

36.

Passing by the summoning of the sages (the 'Postillions' Sinfonia brings them with a team of prancing fillies), their incompetence and discomfiture, we arrive at the intervention of Daniel who, first angry at the dangled rewards in the eye-flashing deliberation of

37.

deals with the writing on the wall in a recitative of vast suggestibility. The antiquity in the Gregorian aspect of

38.

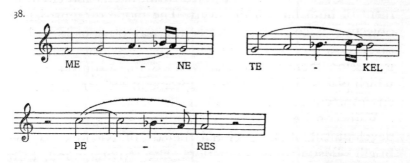

is probably accidental—unless Handel had changed his mind since writing to Mattheson on the subject of modes—but

Daniel's reply to Nicotris, anxious about her son and inquiring about his possible conclusions, commences deliberately with a compact Mixolydian progression.

Affection for *Belshazzar* must lie, however, not in the quality of individual numbers but in the comprehensiveness of the whole. Singers naturally judge Handel from one angle—the virtuoso. This is a mistake for the songs in such a work as this are expressive of facets of personality and the rounded character can only fully be understood when the sum of that character's music is assimilated.

Belshazzar himself is a cheerful rogue, irresponsible but not unattractive. There is in his composition something of the fatality of the House of Stuart. Cyrus is efficient, confident and humane. The two airs addressed to the Almighty, 'Great God! who yet but darkly known' and 'O God of Truth' wear a comfortable cloak of self-assurance and self-satisfaction. Against the single-mindedness of Cyrus may be set the sophistry of Daniel and the devotion of that early fifth-columnist Gobrias. These characters, the bad king, the good king, the soothsayer, the courtier, were the stock in trade of every opera. But pre-eminent in the company stands the tragic queen-mother, Nicotris.

Handel was no esoteric and his characterization, like that of Scott, was from the outward form, habits and environment of humanity to the heart. The mode of approach is objective. Nicotris therefore is in a way obvious as Isolde, say, is not. But there is gain rather than loss, for while there is passion there is also clarity. It is this exquisite clarity which places Handel's music supreme in the period and the environment to which it belonged.

With conciseness in expression comes epigram and the development of the personal tragedy of Nicotris may be briefly illustrated by quotation. The striving mind, torn between mother love and religious duty, throws off immediately after the anti-imperialistic prologue this anxious

phrase, in which the touch of poignancy comes from the
unusual use of the leading note.

39.

Midway in the revels of Belshazzar Nicotris delivers herself
of a homily against licentiousness. Virtuosity (for
Francesina's benefit) ties up with drama in a brilliant
portrayal of mental turmoil. A chance resemblance in one
detail to the 'Confutatis' of the Mozart *Requiem* throws even
more relevance into the experience of the music.

40.

The duet 'O dearer than my life' has again a Mozartian tinge. Here the maternal tenderness of Nicotris and the thematic development of the music expand in the general direction of sonata form. The tendency to regard the Handelian cadence as an inevitable and tiresome cliché leads contemporary performers, devoid of either the freedom or the ability to extemporize as Handel's own singers did, to ignore the latent possibilities of subtlety in emphasis. The tired conclusion of 'Alternate hopes and fears' may speak for itself.

41

find,   my wea-ry   soul no   rest   can   find.

And finally the queen in spacious dignity subordinates personal grief to a care for the welfare of her people in a moving dialogue with Cyrus—'Great victor'.

The first audience to hear *Belshazzar* were critical of the singers—Francesina, Miss Robinson, Beard, and Reinhold. Such criticism may not have been unjust, for this is music which demands not only ability to sing but also that most rare capacity for being able to act with the voice. We shall never appreciate Handel in England until we get rid of the heresy that there exists a peculiar creature designated as an 'oratorio' singer. Handel exercised a catholic choice of singers. Since Handel's time puritanism has won at every turn. And so, while our singers are perverted by popular opinion, the best of the oratorios, including *Belshazzar*, remain a clandestine delight to a tutored minority. This was not the intention behind their creation.

Chapter Nine

OCCASIONAL WORKS

THE *General Advertiser* for 31 January, 1746, bore this advertisement:

We hear that Mr Handel promises to exhibit some musical entertainments, on Wednesdays or Fridays the ensuing Lent, with the intent to make good to the subscribers that favoured him last season the number of performances he was not then able to complete. In order thereto, he is preparing *A* NEW *Occasional Oratorio*, which is designed to be performed at the Theatre Royal, in Covent Garden.

It will be remembered that in the early part of 1745 Handel fell into a state of mental and physical depression. *Belshazzar* went over the heads of the majority of his patrons who, to show their disapproval, stayed away from the remaining oratorios of the year. Then, once again, ill health supervened. It would appear likely that the old trouble of 1737 recurred and that a year of inactivity was caused by the slow process of recovery from a second seizure. But in the old man there were still hidden reserves of power.

Neither the *Occasional Oratorio* nor *Judas Maccabaeus* gave much hint of the remaining stores of sublimity, but their creation served to recall Handel to his proper occupation. Behind them was the stimulus of military success; they were designed as a copious, national *gratias agimus*—to God and to the Duke of Cumberland. Whether the former felt gratified at the ascription to Him of the effectiveness of the slaughterous exploits of the latter at Culloden may be doubted, but history coldly observes what the eye of contemporaneity missed.

The military history of the eighteenth century is conveniently catalogued within the impressive list of Handel's occasional music—an inventory which serves to underline the utilitarian basis of much eighteenth century music. The termination of the War of Spanish Succession (1713) produced the Utrecht *Te Deum;* the fortunate outcome of the battle of Dettingen (1743) a similar offering (with Prussia on the wrong side and a brother-in-law intimately associated with the Prussian War Ministry, Handel must have suffered some afflicting mental difficulties, for he never forgot his native loyalties); the progress of the insurgent clansmen from the Highlands provoked the hortatory Handel to a temporarily popular song for the Gentlemen Volunteers; Culloden was celebrated with two vast votes of thanks; and the end of the War of Austrian Succession in the Peace of Aix-la-Chapelle (1749) evoked the noisy effusion of the *Music for the Royal Fireworks.*

Handel himself felt that posterity would exalt his more indifferent music at the expense of his best. 'How do you like it?' he said to Mr Fountayne, as they sat together in Marylebone Gardens engulfed by the massive sounds of the Handel-tuned band. 'It is not worth listening to', replied the other, oblivious of the paternity of the offending music— or else inspired with a combative bout of intellectual honesty, 'it is very poor stuff.' 'You are right, Mr Fountayne it is very poor stuff. I thought so myself when I had finished it.' Or again: 'A gentleman whom he had desired to look over *Judas Maccabaeus* having declared his opinion of it, "Well", said Handel, "to be sure you have picked out the best songs, but you take no notice of that which is to get me all the money", meaning the worst in the whole oratorio.' And about the merits of *Messiah* we read in Morell's records

of Handel's greater affection for *Theodora*. 'Handel himself,
valued it more than any performance of the kind, and when
I once asked him, whether he did not look upon the Grand
Chorus in *The Messiah* [*sic*] as his Masterpiece? "No", says
he, "I think the chorus at the end of the second part in
Theodora far beyond it, 'He saw the lovely Youth' ".'

Dr Morell (1703-84) was, like most of Handel's literary
coadjutors, regarded with less than respect in literary circles,
but he had many points which would commend him to the
composer. He was 'a warm friend and a cheerful companion
who loved a jest, told a good story and sang a good song'.
He lived at Turnham Green with Thomson, Garrick, and
Hogarth as neighbours and didn't appear to resent noctur-
nal calls from Handel (if report may be trusted) regarding
verbal definitions. In addition to his personal attractiveness
and his scholarship, which was not negligible, Morell had
a good working knowledge of music. On this account he
was requested in 1746 to preach the sermon at the Three
Choirs Festival. His affection for the organ was memorialized by Hogarth who, in 1762, drew Morell 'in the character
of a cynic philosopher, with an organ near him'.

Morell dealt with the libretto for *Judas Maccabaeus* but the
Occasional Oratorio required less attention from a professional
librettist. The text is biblical or Miltonic and thus suggests
a particular personal Handelian touch. The third part of the
oratorio borrowed extensively, and effectively, from *Israel
in Egypt*. The first two parts, despite some recasting of
material from *Athaliah*, were new. Because the *Occasional
Oratorio* was more obviously topical than any other work
by Handel its fame (except for the overture, which is a
programme builder's stand-by) declined as the events which
it celebrated receded into the distances of time. This is
regrettable, for there is much that is monumental in the
work. Unfortunately there is no plot.

The first bass aria, 'Why do the Gentiles' is a variant,
imaginatively speaking, of 'Why do the nations' and

contained in it is the same dignity of fury. The first part cul-
minates in a magnificent and eloquent hymn of praise,
'Jehovah is my strength and shield', which shows something
of the growing simplicity of Handel's aria statements and
something of affinity with hymnody. The tune 'Hanover'
which has been ascribed to Handel would appear to spring
from the same stock. There is at least one other really
magnificent aria, designed for Reinhold, 'To God our
strength sing loud and clear' which whips the chorus into a
festival anthem, based on the bell motive which appears in
very different circumstances in the 'Envy' chorus of *Saul*.

The *Occasional Oratorio* was plain propaganda. The chorus
implores the Almighty—for the second time in Handelian
oratorio—to 'bless the church, and save the king'. It further
exhorts the loyal that 'with pious united hearts [a sustained
A in the middle parts parallels the 'rock' suggestiveness of
the same device in the 'Hallelujah' chorus of *Messiah*] we all
will conquer'. Two phrases from 'When warlike ensigns
point the way rather deliberately to the patriotism of Arne.
But the aria is worth more than this reference for the middle
section does not fail to mention the sordid and terrible
depredations of military affairs on those of agriculture.
Handel turns the eye of compassion on the 'frighted
peasant' and the flockless fields call forth a distant vision of
pastoral quiet.

42.

pas - ture new   the plain af - fords.

To suggest that Cumberland deserved 'The sword that's
drawn in virtue's cause' is to overrate that prince's morals,
while the conclusiveness of Beard's

> *Tyrants whom no cov'nants bind, nor solemn oaths can awe*
> *Strove to enslave the free-born mind, religion, liberty, and law.*

leads to dangerous simplification. But Handel really believed what he wrote. He was, although in earlier days he
had had many near-Jacobite friends, a loyalist. He was also
a fervent admirer of the English system of government:
'he would often speak of it as one of the great felicities of
his life that he was settled in a country where no man
suffers any molestation or inconvenience on account of his
religious principles'.

The *Occasional Oratorio*, first performed on February 14,
1746 was an interim vote of thanks. The rebels had been
sent packing, but their final annihilation was not until
April—and so we come, in point of time, to the origins of
Judas Maccabaeus.

The *Morning Herald* (19 February, 1852) commented:
'The airs of *Judas Macchabaeus*, like those in many other works
of Handel, are occasionally FEEBLE and INSIPID, but
two or *three* of them are exactly the reverse, and, *in the hands*

of singers of ability BECOME both *important* and *interesting.'*
For which excellent exhibition of critical judgement in a
generally uncritical age the anonymous correspondent was
lambasted by the affronted Schoelcher. 'If', he writes,
'Dante had been acquainted with the author of that article,
he would have put him into the hottest place in his *Inferno.'*
Handel, one suspects, would have readily filled that department with rows of self-satisfied sycophants.

The decline into claptrap, experienced in *Judas Maccabaeus*,
is a disease common to Poets Laureate and Masters of the
King's Music when pushed to work. *Judas Maccabaeus* is
made for one hearing. Unfortunately, by some curious
accident (presumably the matter of simplicity actuates the
general run of oratorio promoters), this oratorio runs second
only to *Messiah* in popularity. Which means that one un-
representative and one mediocre work are taken as typical
examples of Handel's style. It is difficult to see how the
mock heroism of 'We come in bright array' (Sullivan had
this sort of thing in mind when he Handelized his Cornish
police force) and the succeeding complaisance of half a
dozen other choruses in which Israelitish bellicosity is
pictured, get past any sober artistic judgement. They merely
serve to recall the pretence of operatic mock militarism. The
Occasional Oratorio is infinitely more real in suggestion.

There are, however, two exceptional choruses—'Mourn
ye afflicted children' and 'For Zion lamentation make'. For
the *Occasional Oratorio* Handel had levied contributions from
Israel in Egypt. The opening mood of the earlier work
accords with the emotions of the unfortunate Israelites who,
before the acknowledgement of the leadership of Judas
Maccabaeus, were repining the death of Mattathias. Thus we
are again plunged into the gloom of C minor. The first
chorus exemplifies the certitude of Handel's phrasing. It is
the shape of his terse subjects which gives point to his
counterpoint. Skill in manipulation is useless unless there
is something to manipulate. Phrases such as

are representative and familiar. At the same time they are malleable to the hand of the technician.

The heavy pageantry of the funereal observations displays German antecedents and we momentarily see Handel in the same line as was continued later by Schumann, Brahms, and Wagner. There is in *Israel in Egypt*, in the Funeral Anthem, in *Samson*, in *Saul*, and in *Judas Maccabaeus* a gloomy pleasure in mortuary musing. But, however one may feel the ominous beat of masochistic romanticism, there is no doubt of the power of Handel's chromatics. The second chorus of the first scene carries in its harmonies an immense feeling of dramatic tension. One quotation will suffice.

words   that weep,   and   tears   that speak

It is not for these numbers that the work is held in affectionate esteem but for the jingling strains and careless rapture of arias of little intrinsic merit. These may be left to the attention of competitors at musical festivals and for the better furnishing of other pious orgies.

By accident *Judas Maccabaeus*, which was meant to celebrate the successful outcome of a military campaign, caught the enthusiasm of the London Jewish community. So for his next two oratorios Handel chose texts designed to work on the same enthusiasm. The amiable Morell prepared a pedestrian libretto on the subject of Alexander Balus.

At this point we may draw aside to examine the polarity of Handel's nature. One aspect of his imagination turned north toward the solemnity of middle class virtue and toward the homiletic; another faced south toward the geniality of sunny grace and Italian charm. The matter of adapting mediterranean art forms to the punctilio of Anglo-Saxon prudery is one which had been of concern to other artists. Hence the reduction of the practice of Bramante and Bernini and the theory of Vitruvius to the parochial architecture of Wren, Hawksmoor, Vanbrugh, and Gibb. At worst the result is dull; at best whimsicality overtops competence. So it was with Handel. *Judas Maccabaeus* is dull, although the efficiency of workmanship may not be questioned. *Alexander Balus* is a poem.

Handel's sense of orchestral colouring is nowhere better illustrated than in this work, the purpose of which is to present familiar problems in unfamiliar light. We have a story of ambition and unscrupulousness and, interwoven, a tale of true love. After dealing with many similar themes in the course of his operatic life, Handel might well have taken the bare outline of the plot for granted, but he was fascinated—like a good Romantic—by the overall influence of the mysterious Middle East. Alexander Balus was king of Syria, Ptolemy, king of Egypt. Thus, before arriving at any sort of musical plan Handel promised himself appropriate richness in local colour. The 'Chorus of Asiates' are introduced by the full panoply of oboes, bassoons, horns, drums and strings and harpsichord (or organ). It will be also noted that the heathen are released from the bondage of music cast in ecclesiasticism. Their choruses are swift, direct, tuneful, often running in octaves like the music of the court of Belshazzar, operatic and melodramatically impressive. The ubiquitous Israelites make due and dutiful appearance but the element of religion is redundant. After the kidnapping of Cleopatra, Jonathan himself, leader of the Jews, temporarily comes to this conclusion:

The creature Gods he trusteth can not help:
They are no Gods, but mere delusion all.

The centre piece of the oratorio is Cleopatra and around her person is set some of Handel's loveliest designs. Her first aria, in which she awakens to her love for Alexander—'Hark! He strikes the golden lyre'—moves in the embrace of two flutes, strings, with the cellos divided and the basses pizzicato, harp and mandoline. In the garden scene—a scene which has precedent in the operas—muted strings and pizzicato cellos set us dreaming 'amid the shady woods'. This is the scene which is rudely interrupted by the hired ruffians of Ptolemy. They break in to seize the person of Cleopatra. In modern parlance this is to create an 'incident'. Ptolemy, ambitious to unite the kingdoms of Egypt and Syria, spares no pains to force Alexander to fight. But before

the method direct comes the insidious technique of below-
stairs whispering. Alexander is made suspicious of Jonathan.
And here we return to a theme already treated in *Saul*.

The 'calumny' chorus, treading heavily on this introductory passage in octaves

45.

shows Handel so far forgetting himself as to allow rhythm
entirely to defeat harmony. The bass goes on, inexorably
on, and discord of a new nature arises when static chorus
and moving bass find such divergence in their ways—

46.

Ptolemy, as presented in this oratorio is a startlingly modern
ruler, even to the extent of having up his sleeve Demetrius
to replace Alexander as puppet monarch of the acquired
province. It is not, perhaps entirely relevant but as Handel

L

wrote *Alexander Balus*, Frederick the Great was practising the act of faith by which he believed that 'the interests of the State ought to serve as the rule to monarchs'. His first victim was Maria Theresa.

Handel gives us much that is topical. Besides the roguery of politics he shows that public persons can have no private lives. The real love of Cleopatra and Alexander lives in a moment's dream. No sooner are they married — and the exaltation of marriage shaped into floral beauty with such exquisite cross-accentation as

— than the tempest of trouble begins to blow up. In the end death removes both husband and father and Cleopatra is left to the ministrations of the god-fearing Jonathan. Handel looks behind the scene and proposes as the great healing influence the benign power of nature. So, when Jonathan praises the 'God who made the radiant sun',

Handel flies with relief to the pageant of the heavens. His translucent music, arching in gentle arpeggio quavers over the anchoring quietude of a tonic pedal, rises to a Wordsworthian reverence.

Before we leave this collection of works associated with Morell (we return to him later) reference may be made to his biographical asides. These illuminate the working scene.

And now as to Oratorios [he writes in a letter some time after Handel's death]. There was a time (says Mr Addison) when it was laid down as a maxim, that nothing was capable of being well set to Musick, that was not nonsense. And this, I think, though it might be wrote before Oratorios were in fashion, supplies an Oratorio-writer (if he may be called a writer) with some sort of apology; especially if it be considered, what alterations he must submit to, if the composer be of an haughty disposition, and has but an imperfect acquaintance with the English language. As to myself, great lover as I am of music, I should never have thought of such an undertaking (in which, for the reasons above, little or no credit is to be gained) had not Mr Handel applied to me when at Kew in 1746, and added to his request the honour of a recommendation from Prince Frederick. Upon this I thought I could do as well as some who had gone before me, and within two or three days carried him the first act of *Judas Maccabaeus*, which he approved of. 'Well', says he, 'and how are you to go on?' 'Why, we are to suppose an engagement, and that the Israelites have conquered, and so begin with a chorus as "Fallen is the foe", or something like it.' 'No, I will have this', and began working it, as it is, upon the harpsichord. 'Well, go on.' 'I will bring you more tomorrow.' 'No, something now.' 'So fall thy foes, O Lord—' 'That will do', and immediately carried on the composition as we have it in that most admirable chorus. That incomparable air, 'Wise men, flattering, may deceive us' (which was the last he composed, as 'Sion now his head shall raise' was his last chorus) was designed for *Belshazzar*, but that not being performed, he happily flung it into *Judas Maccabaeus*. N.B.—The plan of *Judas Maccabaeus* was designed as a compliment to the Duke of Cumberland, upon his returning victorious from Scotland. I had introduced several incidents more apropos, but it was thought they would make it too long, and they were therefore omitted. . . .

And now regarding the next oratorio.

The next year, [writes Morell], he desired another, and I gave him *Alexander Balus*, which follows the history of the foregoing in the Macabees. In the first part there is a very pleasing air, accompanied with the harp, 'Hark, hark, he strikes the golden lyre!': in the second two charming duets, 'O what pleasure past expressing' and 'Hail, wedded love, mysterious law'. The third begins with an incomparable air in the affetuoso style, intermixed with the chorus recitative that follows it. And as to the last air I cannot help telling you that when Mr Handel first read it he cried out, 'Damn your iambics!' 'Don't put yourself in a passion, they are easily trochees!' 'Trochees, what are trochees?' 'Why, the very reverse of iambics, by leaving out a syllable in every line, as instead of "Convey me to some peaceful shore", "Lead me to some peaceful shore".' 'That is what I want.' 'I will step into the parlour and alter them immediately.' I went down and returned with them altered in about three minutes, when he would have them as they were, and had set them most delightfully, accompanied with only a quaver and a rest of three quavers.

Morell was not disinclined to stress the quality of his contribution but the reader may understand sympathetically that the public more often than not ignored the librettist entirely. Moreover Handel's brusqueness was sometimes stimulant to authors' conceit. 'What, you teach me music', he said to Morell one day after the latter had ventured some point of musical criticism, 'The music, sir, is good music. It is your words is bad. Hear the passage again. There! go you and make words to that music.'

Joshua, intended as a companion work to *Judas Maccabaeus*, suffers unjust neglect. It is wholesome, unified and grateful in performance, contains much less than its companion work of mechanical laudation, is varied in aspect and has a sustained vigour in the choral narrative. At the same time one cannot help but feel about the heroic oratorio what Gustav Holst experienced in reading the stories from which the oratorio plots were taken. 'I wanted to read the minor prophets but found there was too much Hitler in them for my taste.' Joshua, in particular, is almost insufferable. However, the intrinsic inspiration comes from sources other

than the character of the hero himself. With him we are
never in sympathy as we are with Saul, Samson, and Jephtha.

Something of the fragrance of *Alexander Balus* overhangs
the middle pages of *Joshua*. We are thrown into the pretty
atmosphere of pastoral love with Othniel and Achsah. Less
intoxicating than the *liebestraum* music of *Orlando* and less
topographically particular than the enchantment of *L'Allegro*,
the concluding pages of the first part, nevertheless, hold
a tremulous grace. After the city's crowded clamour we
are neatly refreshed

> *In these blest scenes, where constant pleasure reigns,*
> *And herds and bleating flocks adorn the plains;*
> *Where the soft season all its blessings sheds,*
> *Refreshing rivers, and enamell'd meads . . .*

Thereunto, after the manner of all shepherds and shepherd-
esses of classical birth and idyllic upbringing, resort Othniel
and Achsah. But, so far as the music is concerned, they retire
with discretion in favour of the linnet and the thrush, who
thus

join their song to the pellucidity of an irrelevant, but
delicious, afternoon. Othniel is, however, a warrior and the
course of love is irrupted by the call of duty. With a
symbolic summons to arms (a recitative motivated by the
customary martial arpeggio of D major) Othniel proceeds
to the destruction of Jericho, emboldened by a spacious
and hortatory chorus, 'May all the host of heaven'.

At this point we catch up with Joshua, who has—to his
surprise—received angelic commission to obliterate the city.
The march from *Joshua* is familiar: it is the worst music in
the oratorio. The scenes of destruction, detailed with infallible precision, flash through the music with the vividness
of a documentary film. The exultation of the military, the
tense enthusiasm of the leader exude from the solo *cum*
chorus treatment of the 'Glory to God'. From pomp and
circumstance the movement proceeds to reality:

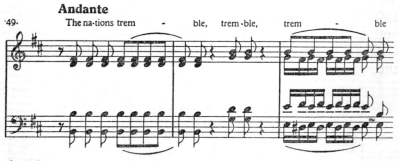

the elements enter the fray:

'the strong cemented walls, the tott'ring towers, the pond'rous ruin falls', and the orchestra makes final comment:

The first operation is followed by another of similar proportions. The kings of the Ammonites are routed by Joshua, or rather by Joshua aided by suspension of the natural laws: sun and moon conveniently, at his behest, stand still during the course of the battle. Again a magniloquent solo *cum* chorus deals graphic strokes of proportionate grandeur. The efficiency of the military draws alarming attention to the satisfaction which atavism generally finds in total destruction. The division of the conquered lands by

Joshua is again memorial to the endless pattern of might triumphant over right. Passing by the narrative (Handel studied his plots and underlined what appeared to merit emphasis) and its moral we arrive at the contemplation of Caleb.

The theme of *secura quies* is calmly and affectionately embroidered in the rounded serenity of 'Shall I in Mamre's fertile plain'. This music

52.

not only bears a poetic contentment in an ordered domain but a patrician ripeness evocative of mellowed age. The succeeding chorus of praise falls relevantly into the character of the air. This deference of choral utterance is the art by which, in his best works, Handel achieves homogeneity.

Othniel deals with a further pocket of resistance, returns to the laurel wreath and the entwining jubilation of 'See the conqu'ring Hero comes', is greeted by Achsah, irresistible with 'Oh! had I Jubal's lyre' (drawn on the account of the juvenile *Laudate pueri*) and vanishes from sight amid the plaudits of the crowd. Great Jehovah is finally brought back as 'our awful theme', but the pious epode is anticlimactic to the gregarious merrymaking.

Chapter Ten

SOLOMON AND SUSANNA

THE tally for the summer of 1748 was, so far as Handel was concerned, one historical essay inspired also with the excitement of a traveller's tale and one novel in disguise—*Solomon* and *Susanna*. The one, fittingly, a large work, the other, equally fittingly, a relatively slender work. The first echoed in solemnity the hopes of those who anticipated that—and here there was particular reference to the opportunities afforded by the Governors of the Foundling Hospital—English art should grow great on the nourishment of history; the second glanced not too indirectly at the moral bias of the contemporary novel. *Clarissa* appeared in 1747-8 and Fielding, just elected to the magistracy, was promising *Tom Jones* for 1749.

Solomon exalts reason, wisdom, wealth, and cultured ostentation: the proper work for a nation on the point of satisfactory emergence, thanks to the Pelham administration, from protracted war, the Peace of Aix-la-Chapelle being finally signed in October 1748, and within sight of imperial greatness and commercial omnipotence. The *Occasional Oratorio* and *Judas Maccabaeus* are more obviously topical but *Solomon* must be regarded in spirit as complementary.

'Handel', writes Paul Lang, 'glorified the rise of the free people of England in his oratorios. The people of Israel become the prototype of the English nation, the chosen people of God reincarnated in Christendom, and magnificent Psalms of thanksgiving and marches of victory in imperial baroque splendour proclaimed the grandiose consciousness of England's world-conquering power . . .' *Solomon* is the last but not the least in the series of heroic and gratulatory musical celebrations in the form of oratorio. In many ways it is the finest of Handel's pageant displays. The vehicle for pageantry is the choir (orchestral subtlety is more useful in other works of a more intimate and speculative nature) and the memory of the great celebratory choruses rings on.

From the censer curling rise
Grateful incense to the skies;
Heav'n blesses David's throne
Happy, happy Solomon.
Live for ever, pious David's Son,
Live for ever, mighty Solomon.

Thus the courtiers applaud their king at the beginning of the second part of the oratorio, that which portrays in particular the personal qualities of the monarch. And the section ends in similar mood—the music now declining, to be truthful, to the lower levels of middle-class pomp and circumstance:

Swell the full chorus to Solomon's praise,
Record him, ye bards, as the pride of our days,
Flow sweetly the numbers that dwell on his name,
And rouse the whole nation in songs to his fame.

It is impossible to believe other than that the intention was to read George for Solomon throughout. George II was the hero of Dettingen, the patron of the Foundling Hospital, to which he gave £2,000 and an additional £1,000 for the inauguration of instruction for the children in the principles

of the Christian religion, the friend of Handel and the symbol of the victory of constitutional government over the
forces of insurrection and reaction. From the architectural
point of view the first part of the oratorio came in usefully
in support of the funds at that time being collected for
the erection of the Foundling Hospital chapel.

The spirit of *Solomon* accords with that of the patriotic
sentiments of Purcell—*King Arthur* was in similar vein
propagandist—and, indeed, looks behind Purcell to the
glittering tributes laid by Lulli at the feet of Louis XIV and
to the gracious flamboyance of the Stuart masque. The last
act of the oratorio is, in fact, an affluent parade in the manner,
mutatis mutandis, of a masque. Samuel Johnson—the great
Chams of literature and of music overlapped in more than
the mere matter of date—contained within a work published
in the same year as that in which *Solomon* appeared the
picture which Handel presented:

> *the pride of awful state,*
> *The golden canopy, the glitt'ring plate,*
> *The regal palace, the luxurious board,*
> *The liv'ried army, and the menial lord.*

All this we have seen in *Athaliah* and in *Belshazzar*, but
there was opulence combined with barbarism. *Solomon* holds
the gorgeous East in fee by implication, but the note of
rationalism sounds throughout.

Handel allows no precedents of style or outlook to con-
fuse his imagination; therefore each work, however superficially similar to another, is complete in independence.
Solomon is the more imaginative because the fertile imagination is restrained within the limits of conscious design.
It is this sense of overall design combined with fitness for
the climax of particular historic circumstances which ensures
that *Solomon* is classical in outlook. In its tidy grandeur, in
its economy and precision, in its cultured aspiration towards

pure beauty it is evocative of that part of its age which is enshrined in contemporary architecture and book design. *Susanna,* on the other hand is fundamentally romantic. None the less, like *The Rape of Lucretia* which also deals with the assault of lust on chastity, it is a morality. This fitted it more for the intellectual comprehension of contemporary dramatic and literary thought than for the stern and unbending propriety of the puritanically religious. *Susanna* would have attracted Edward Moore, whose *The Foundling* had been performed at Drury Lane in the February of 1748.

Brooke's prologue to this play indicates the tendency which Handel, as a connoisseur of the theatre, could hardly have missed.

> *He forms a Model of a virtuous Sort,*
> *And gives you more of Moral than of Sport;*
> *He rather aims to draw the melting Sigh,*
> *Or steal the pitying Tear from Beauty's Eye;*
> *To touch the Strings, that humanize our Kind,*
> *Man's sweetest strain, the Musick of the mind.*

It is relevant to mention that Handel on one occasion mentioned to Lord Kinnoul his didactic purpose and on another he excused the relative failure of *Theodora* by reference to its Christian story (which kept the Jews away) and its morality (which gave displeasure to the ladies). Morality and music made a late marriage in the career of Handel but there is no doubting that he did change his personal outlook so as to approve this union. And so we draw on to the standards of the Victorians, but neither Handel nor Moore would have been content to horizon their view with prudery. Thus *The Foundling* and *Susanna* fell from grace. Edward Moore is no direct concern of ours but Handel is and the oblivion from which *Susanna* has never been rescued must be lamented.

Solomon also fell from favour and the only possible

explanation lies in the fact that it was regarded as a topical work, as indeed it was. The choralist may generally be castigated for neglect in respect of Handel's music. When he (or she) leaves the confines of familiarity he will meet chorus after chorus with similar rapture to that displayed by the Sacred Harmonic Society on their revival of *Solomon* in 1845: 'its auditors were quite unprepared for the beauty of these splendid choruses, some of which have, more recently, been repeated with triumphant success at the Handel Festivals at the Crystal Palace'.

Now *Solomon* may be commended for its choruses as *Susanna* for its airs and dialogues but, paradoxically, the best music in the oratorios comes in the solos in the first and in the choruses in the second. So Handel understood the problem of balance and proportion in extended works. The most effective passages in *Solomon* are, in one way, irrelevant. The one concerns the characterization of the two litigant women while elsewhere the attention is persistently caught by the demonstrative affection for nature displayed both by Solomon and Handel.

The scene which brings the two claimant mothers before the king delineates unerringly the characters of the women and herein Handel offers great scope to singers who are at the same time actresses. From the musical point of view the true and the false are distinguished by rhythmic contrast: thus the true mother, hesitatingly, sadly—

53.

Words are weak to paint my fears: Heart-felt an - guish, start - ing tears

and the wanton, garrulous, plausible, zealous in over-statement.

Solomon, judicially succinct, maintains in this trio a
steady (and slightly monotonous) burden apt in contour to
the non-committal 'Justice holds the lifted scale'. After the
pronouncement that the babe should be divided the second
woman combines satisfaction, flattery, and forwardness
within the impertinence of

to which her rival replies in the tragic beauty of 'Can I see
my infant gor'd', of which the concluding bars carry this
cadence

The devices, of broken melody, of chromatic gesture, of suspension, and of anxious rhythmic pulsation in the bass, are all obvious but undeniably effective and timely. The conclusion of the scene 'Thrice blest be the king' is a duet between the first woman and the king, calling for no comment other than that Solomon still maintains the scale phrase which he proposes in the opening movement of this scene. This is the only moment of high tension, of interplay between rough and opposing forces—the root of dramatic climax—in the oratorio, and it is a fine example of Handelian analysis.

There is, despite his magnificence, something pathetic about Solomon, as indeed there must always be about the man apotheosized to the dignity of kingship. Solomon in all his glory makes a tawdry show by the side of the lily of the field. More or less unconsciously Handel (and his librettist) underline the significance of this entirely Romantic thought and the king is shown at his happiest when away from his entourage and amid rusticity. Here too we see another facet of Handel himself, the urbanite with wistful affection for the quietude of country retreat.

With his queen, Solomon hastes to the cedar grove and listens to the turtle doves, the amorous turtles who had already made appearance in *Acis and Galatea*. Then to the unsheltered moor. Zadok, the priest, at a later point in the oratorio, admires the tall palm while the first woman sinking back—again the emotional decrescendo of thought shows a capacity for realization of the exact processes of mental behaviour—into the tranquillity of longed-for peace of mind, enchants the air with the serenity of the *pastorale* 'Beneath the vine'. This country song catches the atmosphere of 'Let me wander not unseen' from *L'Allegro* and echoes the exquisite delicacy of John Dyer's 'The Country Walk'. The moral too is the same:

> *Happy swain, sure happier far*
> *Than lofty kings and princes are!*

Nor does Solomon omit to point out to the Queen of Sheba, a far more alluring creature than his proper queen, the pleasant fertility of his domains. But the moment of richest impressionism comes from the chorus. And here we revert to the first part of the oratorio.

If there is one chorus above all others which demonstrates the necessity for being faithful to Handel's own standards of choral balance it is the sweet, crepuscular 'May no rash intruder'. Here the qualitative timbre of a small choir (a chorus of more than fifty singers inevitably loses character, each part becoming tonally impersonal) and the tact of clear-voiced piano and cantabile phrasing are needed to blend with the illustrative detail of orchestral partnership—for this is no mere matter of accompaniment. The more or less equal balance between voices and instruments leaves us embowered in music as evocative and as English as Elgar's representation of Shallow's orchard. The country refrain is the keynote of English music and poetry alike; in the musical tradition Handel shows here the half-way mark between, say, Wilbye and Weelkes on the one hand and Elgar and Vaughan Williams on the other. The voices carry the flexibility of the madrigal, with like appreciation of the aesthetic possibilities of homophony and polyphony; the orchestra persuades acceptance of the poet's mood:

> *And on the green moss I lay me down*
> *That o'er the root of oak has grown;*
> *Where all is silent, but some flood*
> *That sweetly murmurs in the wood*
> *But birds that warble in the sprays,*
> *And charm e'en silence with their lays.*

We may quote the opening bars of this chorus, the loveliest in the oratorio, and draw attention to the fact that the chorus takes on itself a free ternary shape which indicates how nature may furnish the theme for art and how the artist is finally concerned not with naturalistic pleasantry but with the integrity of artistic expression. Thus the five parts sing lullaby:

M

The 'nightingale' chorus is, of course, operatic by heredi-tary endowment. So it is with the other great choruses of *Solomon*. All are concerned with the theme of pageantry, thus they pronounce their respective parts with clear-edged determination to illumine the person and the property of the complimented monarch. 'Your harps and cymbals sound' sets the pace with unisonal declamation from the basses of both choirs (for this is a double chorus), with a typical and regal canto fermo which strides through the detail of the score with sublime theocratic bearing, with rever-berated chords from the alternate choir as from the domed recesses of some great Palladian palace. So also it is with the ardent movement 'With pious hearts', the ritualistic and optative 'From the censer curling rise', the caparisoned 'Shake the dome', the hortatory 'Praise the Lord with harp and tongue', and the finale, 'The name of the wicked shall quickly be past'; all are in eight parts, all are festival pieces, in all 'bold Description paints the walls within' and we live in Athens, in Rome, in Jerusalem, and in the newly monu-mental self-consciousness of Georgian London. The familiar music from this oratorio—the entry music for the Queen of Sheba—is no bad index to the prevailing mood.

On the whole the orchestration of *Solomon* is simple, two flutes dissolve in mimetic ecstasies in 'May no rash intruder', a single flute sings 'Beneath the vine', the more pungent voice of broad-reeded oboe has an obbligato—countered by *traversieri tutti* (*sic*, which seems to indicate more than two) in the aria 'Will the sun forget to streak' and a full brass ensemble of trumpets and horns, together with the invariable and attendant drums, spreads over the climactic choruses. It may be mentioned that the score accomodates two organ parts, one for each choir.

Susanna is topical as is *Solomon*, but in a different manner. *Solomon* is fundamentally artificial, concerning itself with the facade of evident civilization which creates self-satisfaction: the pride of princes overshadows the poverty of their subjects and the public personage hides the tattered character of the private person. *Solomon* gives the prestige of romantic glory to a court whose scandals, while not without interest, were best left hidden. One can never be sure that Handel's reception of the Queen of Sheba was not intended, sardonically, as a commentary on Georgian paramours. *Susanna* possesses a plot which may be worked out in reality on any day of the week. Handel, like Shakespeare, took the symbolic titles of antiquity for convenience and proceeded to portray the persons of his own environment. The oratorio of *Susanna* is then placed in England as much as is *A Midsummer Night's Dream* and behind the human action lies the perpetual beauty and terror of landscape. In many respects *Susanna* is a repetition of *Acis and Galatea*; the story, though less fabulous and more particular, is similar, pastoralism is common to both, and simplicity of statement married to the charm of poetic delicacy makes the whole work a picture of the heroine. Yet between the two works there is a difference. The earlier is amoral, experimental, and somewhat stiffly ordered in the sylvan ways. *Susanna*, in contrast, is a homily in honour of virtue and against corruptness in high places; it is relieved from sententiousness by the truthful observance of persons and places, the fashion in 1748 being keener on rural appreciation than in the previous generation; it is brought into line with English predilections by having more than an occasional reminiscence of balladry. The light-weight airs of this oratorio, which are its particular charm, point the way to the deftness of Arne. Or maybe it is the other way round, for the song settings for *As you like it* came from 1740 and Handel must have come across them. When Joachim commences—

we are in the world of Arne's fancy and when Handel catches his breath—

'*Angels, ever bright and fair*' (*Theodora*)
in Handel's autograph

we are approaching the delicate sentimentality of the little
world of Miss Austen.

The two elders cry out with the pains of unlawful love
and invoke the genius of the place. Says the first—again we
notice the easy lines of popular song—

60.

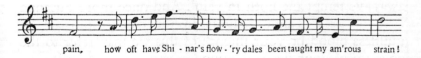

He continues:

> *The wounded Oaks in yonder Grove*
> *Retain the Name of her I love.*

And the oak tree catches the imitative faculty of the second
elder (who at any rate does not appear to have scratched
Susanna on every bole):

> *The oak that for a thousand years*
> *Withstood the Tempest's might,*
> *Like me the darted lightning fears,*
> *And flames with sudden light.*

At which point two bars of super-heated semiquavers together with the tumultuous addition of bassoons distinguish
the virility of this ancient's ardour.

The sterner lines of the oratorio are laid down by the
introductory and ominous chorus 'How long, O Lord'
which rides unexpectedly over this characteristically Purcellian ground:

51.

Then in supreme climax—and to be compared with the
trio in *Solomon*—comes the rebuttal of the elders in 'Away,
away, ye tempt me both in vain'. And once more Susanna
rises to great tragic heights in the court-room air 'If
guiltless blood be your intent': of this we may refer to the
epigram of dour determination

62₁

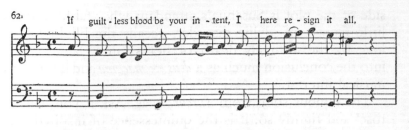

If guilt-less blood be your in-tent, I here re-sign it all,

fear-less of death as in - no-cent, I tri-umph in my fall, I

tri-umph, I tri-umph, I tri-umph in my fall.

and to the change to major tonality by way of calm conclusion. This attitude and behaviour is musically premonitory of Iphis in *Jephtha* and the point must be made (in view of Rockstro's 'insulted matron') that in both cases Handel had in mind young and exquisite creatures. Susanna was made for love and with the adoration of Joachim almost becoming calf-love the tragic parts are made the more impressive, as they are by the idly chattering crowd who await the verdict (in the hope of a pronouncement of guilt) in sibilant gossip.

A word should be spared for Chelsias, who fills his little paternal niche with accustomed dignity and soliloquizes (how all Handel's fathers pray for peace!) serenely in 'Peace, peace, crown'd with roses on your slumbers wait'. At the side of the plot is Susanna's attendant who, faithful to the little fantasy of idyllic disorder, recalls the blight of her love by the untimely death of her swain. Daniel comes into the conclusion much as a *deus ex machina* and holds little musical interest.

The famous song from *Susanna* was 'Ask if yon damask rose' and rightly so: it is the quintessence of inspired simplicity. Such was its individual popularity that it aptly went into *Love in a Village* in 1762 and into the *Lady's Magazine* in 1793.

Solomon and *Susanna* jointly cover many fields of thought. We see in them 'united a most logical head with a most fertile imagination'. And here we may draw on Boswell and transfer to Handel what may equally relate to him as to Johnson.

But his superiority over other learned men consisted chiefly in what may be called the art of thinking, the art of using his mind; a certain continual power of seizing the useful substance of all that he knew, and exhibiting it in a clear and forcible manner; so that knowledge, which we often see to be no better than lumber in men of dull understanding, was, in him, true, evident, and actual wisdom. His moral precepts are practical; for they are drawn from an intimate acquaintance with human nature. His maxims carry conviction; for they are founded on the basis of common sense, and a very attentive and minute survey of real life. His mind was so full of imagery. . . . .

And there the ways divide, for Handel was a poet whereas Johnson was not.

Chapter Eleven

THEODORA AND JEPHTHA

EACH oratorio of Handel has its own specific quality;
each is an essay on some aspect, or aspects, of human
nature. *Theodora*, to which particular attention should be
drawn as being the composer's favourite work in this genre,
is the study of the tragedy of youth and limned with
tenderness, affection, and understanding. At the age of
sixty-five Handel had clearly not forgotten what it was to
feel young and the sympathy of his philosophy might
reasonably appear to have had some stimulus in current
social welfare activity.

. . . the Prince and Princess of Wales, with a great number of
persons of quality and distinction, were at the Chapel of the Foundling
Hospital, to hear several pieces of vocal and instrumental music
composed by George Frederick (*sic*) Handel Esq, for the benefit of
the foundation. 1st The music of the late Fire Works, and the anthem
on the Peace. 2nd Select pieces from the oratorio of Solomon, relating
to the dedication of the Temple: and 3rd General pieces composed for
the occasion, and applicable to the charity and its benefactors. There
was no collection, but the tickets were at half-a-guinea, and the
audience above a thousand.

The Foundling Hospital was only one, if the most
notable, among numerous monuments of piety and charity
which had their foundation during the eighteenth century.
It is difficult to lay a charge of social indifference against the

contemporaries of Handel when one realizes that before 1745 London was enriched by the inauguration of Guy's, Westminster, St. George's, London, and the Middlesex Hospitals. In general, however, charity and the institution of its memorials depended (this is not really exceptional at any time but demonstrative of the value attached in the eighteenth century to individual exercise) on the humanity of noble figures like Captain Coram, Joseph Hanway, whose province was also the care of children, and General Oglethorpe, whose distinction was less on the field of battle than in the debtors' cells. He was, said the *Gentleman's Magazine*, 'an active and enterprizing man, and had distinguished himself as a friend to the unhappy wretches who were prisoners for debts which it was impossible they should pay, by many speeches in the House of Commons in their favour: he was in every respect qualified for the charitable trust that was reposed in him. . . .' Then it should be remembered that this was the century which could produce a Prime Minister in Walpole who considered—contrary to the trend of popular emotion—that saving lives was a grand and stategic duty. Handel himself was not inconspicuous in private charity. He assisted the widow of his old tutor Zachau, he brought the family Smith out of indigence, he took a charity boy (with not very satisfactory results) into his household, he contributed more than money to the Dublin charities and he affected the cause of the Foundlings so much that he took part in the administration of the Hospital. He was, as one obituary notice charmingly puts it, 'liberal even when he was poor, and remembered his former friends when he was rich'.

The age is put into proper perspective by Trevelyan.

It was no accident that Uncle Toby, the Vicar of Wakefield, Mr Allworthy and Parson Adams were leading characters in English fiction during its first great period. A keener sensitiveness to the needs and sufferings of others, particularly of the poor, was not only reflected but was seen in the philanthropists and in the successive activities of the age—the foundation first of Charity Schools; then of Hospitals; and, in the last years of the century, of Sunday Schools.

The soft lines of *Theodora* distil something of the quality of freely bestowed sympathy. Were the music less accomplished and the work destitute of interpolated humour we might be driven to describing this oratorio as sentimental. But sentimentality and Handel remained strangers. And Morell, watch-dog of the plot once more, had a tradition of his own in literary affairs—a tradition of solemnity, scholarship (or pedantry if you prefer), and pomposity. Morell's characters are immobile as those of Thornhill, or Highmore, or Wills, or even of the student Hogarth. History was then invested with pontificality.

The origin of *Theodora* is demonstrative of the relatively close association of Handel's music with the literature of his period. Morell, in the preface to the book of words, acknowledged his source as *The Martyrdom of Theodora and Didimus*, by Robert Boyle, which was published in 1687. In 1756, incidentally, the story was retold in Butler's *Lives of the Saints*. It might be thought that an obscure episode from the martyrology would prove too esoteric for the generality.

This, in fact, was what happened. Thus we realize how irrelevancies may settle the fate of a musical work of genius. Handel's audiences had been weaned from the mythological to the canonical: from opera to oratorio. On occasion variety had been introduced in those hybrid productions, neither opera nor oratorio nor masque—but something akin to all three, commencing with *L'Allegro*, or even *Acis and Galatea* and continuing to the full glory of *Hercules*. *Theodora* was an oratorio *pur sang*. But its hagiographic origin, its uncomfortable insistence on the ultimate devolution of Christian values in an unchristian world and its seriousness of approach put it out of court. Handel neatly summarized the position: 'The Jews will not come, because it is a

Christian story, and the ladies will not come, because it is a virtuous one'. And it was Handel's favourite work.

Theodora was composed between June 28 and July 31, 1749. It was performed at Covent Garden three times in 1750, on March 16, 21 and 23, to exiguous audiences. Then it was not performed again until five years later.

Handel claimed the concluding chorus of Act II 'He saw the lovely youth' as among his most notable achievements. Viewed objectively it can hardly be accorded such an exalted position. But one is inclined to regard Handel's opinion as coloured by the charitable direction of his personal outlook. The vision of the miraculous resurrection of the widow's son of Nain had appealed to the active humanity of the public benefactor (he was elected a Governor of the Foundling Hospital in May 1750). The richness of Handel's mellowed affection draws his characters into a calm contiguity of spiritual reciprocity. Irene is the perfect *confidante*, the sweetest and least egocentric of all exemplars of this type; Septimius has a musical personality which betokens greater love for Didimus than his lines signify. Valens, representative of imperial and pagan Rome, is magnificent in devotion to high duty and to the prestige of the government which he figures.

The Roman persecution, effected through men of the type of Valens—an admirable person if we read Handel rather than Morell—comes close to contemporary problems. Valens discharged his affairs regardless of any censure other than that which would inevitably follow dereliction from one iota of his commission. Policy was made for him. Septimius, of a lower order, is described quite admirably by Macfarren.

The Roman officer is one of those steady-going old believers, who persevere in the creed of their fathers, because they will not be at the pains of collating its corruption with the purity of a new faith. He has no cruelty toward the Christian sect, but likes the ease of following established order, and gaily obeys commands, even to the execution of believing victims, rather than suffer the inconvenience of disputing

them. He is willing to serve his friend, as shown in his accommodating
him with entrance to Theodora's dungeon; but he takes no step to
save his life or that of the heroine for whom this friend is self-sacrificed.

It was, perhaps, easier to write in that strain in the nineteenth century. For now the position of Valens and Septimius is a subject for daily debate. Handel, with his super-
lative powers of characterization, places before us the
eternal riddle of conflicting loyalties. Victory he accords to
those who suffer for the realization of an ideal.

The festive setting of *Theodora* has the glint of vermeil
appropriate to a Roman carnival. To quote Macfarren again:
'The citizens of the Roman empire are presented as pleasure-
loving, but as finding pleasure in grace and gaiety, certainly
not in ebriety or savage violence.' Not inaptly Handel recalls
the court of Charles II in music which owes much to the
example of Purcell. Here is part of the celebration of Venus.

Queen of   Sum - mer, Queen of   Love,_____   and thou

cloud — com - pel - ling Jove,

The objection to *Theodora* from a practical angle is that its

choruses are relatively few, but it must be recognized that
in such a work the artistic vindication of choral interludes
must rely on appositeness. Except in rare cases—as in *Israel
in Egypt*—the chorus must shift dramatically behind the
principal figures of the drama. Oratorio, like opera, is a
flexible organization and all the component parts must be
interrelative. The desideratum for such an intimate work as
Theodora is a small body of performers, such as Handel himself employed. The Christians have half a dozen choruses.
Each is infected with a lyrical sense that contrasts with the
expectation that Handel must exalt godliness through four-
square anthem-like utterances. 'Come mighty Father' carries
into quiet grandeur the elasticity of aria. Thus sinuously the
music implores the deity at the outset;

the final melismatics

are permeated by a feeling of *magnificat*. The finale, in contrast to the general Allelujah or Amen (or admixture of both), luxuriates briefly in the same fluidity of melancholy movement as does the corresponding chorus in *Acis and Galatea*. That too was a tragedy of youthful love, and Handel,

looking back across the years of experience, comes to the
conclusion that elegy for youth calls not for ceremonious-
ness but for primaveral contemplation and commemoration
of brief beauty.

The lyrical quality of the choruses grows naturally from
the quality of the principal arias. Of these the most eloquent
is Irene's 'As with rosy steps', the perfect artistic example of
the by now almost superannuated 'da capo' form. Handel's
perversity with regard to the customary conventions of
major and minor leads his triumphal climax and declaration
of faith into A minor. Unconsciously, no doubt, an eloquent
suggestion of victory through sacrifice is here imparted to
the music. The 'roral' rustle of dawn is modestly reflected
in the cello figuration: from this aria to Schubert's 'Am
Dorfe' is a long step but the two masters frequently approach
in a similarity of concentrated vision. The scheme is settled
in a fragment of melodic contour. Irene further exemplifies
the practice in her exquisite 'Defend her, heaven,' in which
the declining arpeggio figure (a normal Handelian symbol
of heavenly bliss) contrives gentle oscillation throughout.
Thus this aria opens—note the extreme simplicity of harmonic movement :

night,   so from vir-tuous toil well   borne   raise_____ Thou our hopes of

end · less light

Didimus lives in a fairy world. The love-making is sub-
limated, as in *Romeo and Juliet*, to the plane of pure poetry.
In other oratorios, *Saul*, *Samson*, *Joseph*, *Jephtha*, there is an
obvious, recognizable earthy touch; herein the episodes are
contrived for the enjoyment of the audience. In *Theodora*
sex is screened by an ethereal atmosphere of spiritual sensibility. This, roughly, is what Handel meant when he touched
on the 'virtue' of the oratorio. One may also claim that the
heroism is similarly screened. There is about Didimus none
of the masculine, thoughtless unawareness of danger which
elsewhere passes for courage. Instead there is an elegance,
a delicacy, an almost Grecian poise which, in fact, serves as
foil to the military proportion of the Roman Valens. In the
elegant, rhapsodic entwinement of 'The raptured soul'
Didimus is absorbed in the spirit of love and of beauty and
appears nescient, despite the words he utters (and, if he

N

wills, Handel bends the words to *his* meaning) of death.
Septimius, a soldier accustomed to the operations of rack
and gibbet, counters Didimus's sonneteering with a sober
request to the unknown goddess of pity. The difference
between the two may be epitomized

67.

Didimus is clearly one (despite the sporadic requests
contained within 'With courage fire me') lacking the *dona
corragio* and the Italian fluency of his music, 'Sweet rose and
lily' being typical, is fitting. The tragedy of Didimus and
Theodora lies not in the human problem but in the brief
term of beauty. Didimus and Theodora take eloquent leave
of the world in their final duet, after the manner of Steffani.
There is here much of the undercurrent of *Romeo and Juliet*,
the same eloquent beauty, the same sympathy and as the
two martyrs-elect prepare themselves for their final end we
feel the influence of a 'dateless bargain with death'.

Theodora has the courtliness of an ancient, knightly tale.
And Theodora herself has the detailed sweetness of a

medieval. Handel loved her as men love their ideals of womanhood. She has sympathy from the heart on account of her reticence, her dignity, her fragrant virginity. This, however, is no romantic heroine; she is removed from the spacious ranges of latter-day realism and rests within the calm objectivity of classical idealism. She is a more purely musical than dramatic conception. Hence the disfavour with which she was first greeted. The key points of her martyr's progress are the two best known arias in the work : 'Angels ever bright and fair', with which may be compared that serene aria of Iphis in *Jephtha* 'Brighter scenes I seek above', and 'The pilgrim's home'. Both have the sublimity of inspired simplicity. It is this economy of material which selects Theodora, musically, from the conventional white robes of formalized virginity. The character is individual not so much by reason of what is said as by what is omitted. Another aria of great beauty anticipates *Jephtha* 'O that I on wings could rise', this being antecedent in thought and expression to 'Waft her, angels'. A quotation will suffice to indicate the similarity :

68.

swift·ly sail . . . . ing,

swift - ly sail-ing through the skies,   as   skims the   sil - ver dove!

Theodora must rank artistically among Handel's greater creations. The emotional level is restrained and never rises to high passionate intensity, but the emotional limitations focus attention on the high quality of musical development within the oratorio. The overture steps out of the harpsichord suites, holding no reference to the work to which it belongs and being extended to four movements. Of these the third is named a trio and the last a courante.

It is a great relief to be freed in *Theodora* from the eternal details of tribal warfare: this explains the exclusive lyrical nature of the work.

The beauty of *Theodora* rides into *Jephtha*, but in this last oratorio vaster issues are involved. *Theodora* deals with one facet, *Jephtha* with many. The subject of *Jephtha* is the problem of humanity. It is difficult to escape the conclusion that this is the greatest work of all, the climax of the oratorio which emerged nearly two centuries before from the *Chiesa Nuova*. The theme of *Theodora* was that of resignation to the will of God; but the working out of the moral idea appears, viewed retrospectively from the angle of *Jephtha*, somewhat academic. *Jephtha* is a personal document. The conclusion that fate—or the will of God—must be endured, despite what suffering may be entailed; that the operations of the Almighty are ineluctable; that man is insignificant (yet not without his heroic parts) is arrived at by Handel by the way of his own experience of suffering. It has been seen how the tension of *Saul* and the exaltation of *Israel in Egypt* were

Mrs Cibber, one of Handel's favourite singers—ivory relief, 1729

not unconnected with Handel's state of health in 1739: in 1752 he was going blind. Indeed the fact is noted in the pages of the score. Handel accepted his fate and continued to live as full a life as before the calamity of blindness.

Jephtha might well bear this as text, from Jeremy Taylor:

> To be angry with God, to quarrel with the divine providence by repining against an unalterable, a natural, an easy sentence, is an argument of a huge folly, and the parent of a great trouble: . . . patience makes him his own man, and lord of his own interest and person. Therefore possess yourselves in patience, with reason and religion, and you shall die with ease.

Within the philosophy of the work the *dramatis personæ* are symbolic; Jephtha of doubt turning to security in the recognition of infallibility in divine governance: Storge of rebellion against the incomprehensible: Iphis of ignorance, dismay and final acceptance of destiny. At the same time these are real persons and the detailed characterization is magnificent. Handel's works comprise a portrait gallery of his acquaintances and the immediacy of those before us is compelling. Handel recognized the veneer of picturesqueness and utilized its possibilities in mimesis in order to communicate with his hearers in terms of common currency. But he worked into the heart of his subject and illumined his observations with spiritual and psychological truth.

Jephtha more than any other of the oratorios comes near to being a lesson in moral philosophy. The theme is of resignation to the decrees of God. Thus the climax comes with the chorus 'How dark, O Lord, are Thy decrees'. It was at the end of the first section of this chorus that Handel noted 'Reached here on Wednesday, February 13. Prevented from proceeding on account of the relaxation [altered to 'so relaxt'] of the sight of my left eye.' Here is the strain of personal tragedy. There is in this chorus a recapitulation of moods previously expressed in *Saul*. The second section illustrates the seemingly purposeless pilgrimage of humanity:

the syncopated waywardness of Saul's 'From crime to
crime he blindly goes' furnishes the point of one subject
while the other 'As the night succeeds the day' contrasts by
reason of its dark, chromatically varied, descent. The third
stage promises, in severe fugal exposition 'no certain bliss
. . . on earth below'. But nihilism is not the end of thought.
We must believe in a supernatural ordering of affairs, for
'Order is Heav'n's first law'. Of the being of God Handel
(and the eighteenth century) is not always certain. The
maxim we must obey is this—' Whatever is, is right'.

Thought provokes the conclusion of the philosopher but,
in the case of Handel, there comes the overriding triumph
of emotional sympathy. 'How dark, O Lord . . . ' is the
end of a chapter, not of a book. It terminates the second act
of the oratorio, succeeding with complete and infallible
relevance, Jephtha's desperate 'Deeper and deeper still'. The
third act provides, if not a happy ending at any rate a more
hopeful vision. Jephtha curses the sun—the continuity of
despair from act to act is an artistic necessity—but then
looks beyond the immediate scene with the immortal conviction of spiritual ascension in ' Waft her, angels'. The
concluding chorus, 'Ye sons of Gilead', is no mere rever-
beration of conventional Hallelujahs. It is in celebration of
peace—Jephtha's victory over the Ammonites tends to be
forgotten in subsequent complications—and in commemoration of those 'who fear the Lord'. Viewed aright, that is
with thirty and not three hundred singers in mind, this
chorus becomes lyrical, graduating from a brief allegro

a vote of thanks, to a section wherein treads the
Purcellian ♩ ♩—a frequent Handelian symbol of rural
enjoyment, and finally to a fugue of which the subject

has its ancestry in folk dance. The brightness of D major recalls, in tonality at all events, the opening of the oratorio where penitent Israelites renounce Moloch and Chemosh and return to the worship of Jehovah.

Within this general framework lies the plot proper. While Jephtha is the nominal hero it may reasonably be felt that principal interest centres in the changing character of Iphis. Within two-and-a-half hours we witness, in Handel's most penetrating study in characterization, half a lifetime of experience. Youthful charm, the first fine and careless rapture of early love, an awakening to the desperate parts of life, a heroic preparedness to accept immolation, and a final mellowness of spirit in the harness of superior discipline: all these stages pass by in a sequence of arias which hardly have need of text. In this respect it may be mentioned that years of training as a purveyor of operas had enabled Handel to develop more or less simple and concrete ideas into symbolic musical phraseology suggestive to audiences who forced themselves into an appreciation of works in a language which few of them understood.

The pleasant lines of 'Take the heart you fondly gave' are non-committal: the easy fluency of the duet 'These labours past' leaves Iphis and Hamor unconscious of impending issues and introduces divisions which no doubt entranced audiences in search of polite hedonistic reactions. But the apparent irrelevance is not pointless. The bourrée 'The smiling dawn of happy days' is the apt summary of the inexperienced girl whose knowledge and interest is localized to a commonplace narcissism. With her attendant virgins Iphis extends this mood into a gavotte movement 'Welcome as the cheerful light', in which the returning and victorious Jephtha is greeted. Again the lightness has great dramatic effect. Jephtha's vow was to sacrifice in thanksgiving for victory the first living creature to meet him on his return and the tragedy of the necessary slaughter of an innocent is pointed in musical contrasts.

At this point we become conscious of the powerful personality of Storge. Storge synthesizes a great number of operatic and oratorio characters with whom Handel had deep sympathy. Dejanira and Nicotris are representative, too, of the middle-aged wife and mother to whom catastrophe comes suddenly, terribly, and in defiance of any kindly ordering of human affairs. The Hanoverian queens of England, whose private griefs at unfaithful husbands and wilful sons, at sacrificial marriages of their daughters were public property, may not have been far absent from Handel's mind (he owed much to queenly kindness and interest) when he limned, in uncomfortably positive terms, this series of portraits.

'Open thy marble jaws, O tomb' is superb music and superb drama. But it is the peak of a rising sequence of dramatic statements, each one foretelling, by implication, impending tragedy. The opening phrase of Storge's first aria:

70.

may be contrasted with that of Iphis. The dramatic potentialities of the music are immediately clear. Next we meet the terrible intuition of evil possible to a fiery feminine imagination in 'Scenes of horror, scenes of woe'.

The broken octaves, the uncertain flight, the tonal transitions of this aria may be condensed into two climactic bars:

an exhibition of the pervasive realism of the style.

The quartet 'O spare your daughter', in which Zebul (Jephtha's presumably strong and certainly silent half-brother), Hamor and Storge implore Jephtha, the recalcitrant, to 'recall the impious vow', is the finest ensemble to be discovered in the oratorios. More dramatic than anything in any of the choruses, this quartet has the tension of deriving from interwoven personalities such as elsewhere may be experienced in the operas of Mozart. The quality of the quartet infects the succeeding aria of Iphis: 'Happy they' reflects the deepened stoicism of our heroine. This is where she parts company with Theodora, who never ripened to this dignity. And beyond the darkness there comes the radiant acceptance of divine discipline in the golden strains of 'Brighter scenes I seek above' and 'Freely I to heav'n resign'.

Jephtha emerges in sublimity at two familiar points. Elsewhere, although he is the hub of the plot, events surround him, leaving him with relatively little to say. What he does say is, none the less, pertinent.

There are no loose ends in *Jephtha* and it is the combination of economy with graduated climax which make this the artistic masterpiece in the line of oratorio. What applies to the solo items applies equally to the choruses. The evocation of scene, an important function of the chorus, produces the festival music of the first part, the tempered devotion of the conclusion, the intercessory 'O God, behold our sore distress', the tempestuous involutions of the last chorus of the first part and, above all, the detailed, Dantesque vision of 'cherub and seraphim'. The incandescence of the opening is the musical translation of the

> *O vero sfavillar del santo spiro,*
> *Come si fece subito e candente*
> *Agli occhi miei che vinti nol soffriro!*

It is this perpetual fire of the spirit that embraces Handel's genius and it is to the music, beyond the conventions of mundane texts, that we must look to discover that breadth of outlook which, in an art form adapted for the narrow limits of an English musico-dramatic by-product, links the composer with the great parts of medieval Christendom. Handel, from three years study in Italy, had absorbed that much of Dante which was reflective of Italian culture, religion and sentiment. In the widest sense of the word Handel was catholic: of this the best token is *Jephtha*.

We see Handel at the end of his days blind, philosophic and increasingly judicial in his outlook on men and morals. *Jephtha* was the end of serious composition, but there was a brief sequel. In 1757 Dr Morell prepared an English version of *Il trionfo del tempo e del disinganno*. Fifty years before Handel had set this—even then out of date—morality and it had been received without enthusiasm by a Roman audience. In 1737 an enlarged version, but still in Italian, was produced during the opera season. One can only reckon that Handel went back to the subject again at the very end of his life because the sense of admonition, which appears to influence the later works in general, provoked him to offer as his swan-song an ode on the impermanence of beauty, the frailty of charm, the deceit of pleasure. It is improbable that *The Triumph of Time and Truth* will be revived but there are parts—some of them incorporated from the *Parnasso in Festa*—which deserve at least to be anthologized. Once again it is the matter of rural observation which catches the imagination and we recall the elegantly Weber-like *Jägerlied*, preceded by its flourish of horns and the meadow-sweet fragrance of the evocation of dryads and sylvans. Youth, remarks Handel—as in *Theodora*—is a delight: thus runs his commentatory *rondeau*.

First boys with oboes; next tenors with bassoons; finally *tutti*. It may be remarked, in passing, that the text of this work is Morell's most creditable performance, always elegant, musical and occasionally magnificent in its own right in picturesque allusion. There is something here of the new poetic instinct of Gray—

> *The hand of Time pulls down*
> *The great colossus of the sun,*
> *The stone-built castle, cloud-capt tow'rs . . .*

and here of affection for the pretty gallantry of the idealized Gothic:

> *Here Pleasure keeps her splendid court,*
> *Where all her devotees resort;*
> *And, at her nod, advance*
> *The costly feast, the carol and the dance;*
> *Minstrels, and music, poetry and play;*
> *And balls by night, and manly sports by day.*

In the distance stands Lord Byron.

The last air in the oratorio is of incredible beauty: the voice of Beauty sounds the resignation of Iphis and of Theodora:

> *Guardian Angels, oh, protect me,*
> *And in Virtue's path direct me,*
> *While resigned to Heav'n above*
> *Let no more this world deceive me,*
> *Nor vain idle passions grieve me*
> *Strong in Faith, in Hope, in Love.*

The serene melody, running thus

is countered by oboe obbligato and supported by pulsating strings. This is among the sweetest of Handelian songs and the fact that it could appear both in 1708 and in 1757 declares the unity of the Handelian style and at the same instant the composer's independence of the corrosion of time. He, with Horace, said in effect

Exegi monumentum aere perennius.

Chapter Twelve

ORATORIO SINGERS

NO consideration of the Handelian oratorio would be complete without some rather more than cursory reference to the participating singers. It was in the company of singers that Handel frequently worked out his ideas when both operas and oratorios were in embryonic shape. It was to isolate virtuoso singers from the general ensemble that extensive arias were composed. It was in imitation of singers that trumpets and oboes carried, occasionally, long and exhausting divisions. The audiences paid their entrance money more frequently to enjoy the spectacle and the sound of talented singers than to appreciate the fine points of a particular composition. Singers ruled the age—as Addison, Fenton, Hogarth, Carey, Gay, and Smollett indicate in their several ways—and, accordingly, their personalities, their technique, and their respective relations with Handel call for observation.

As there are on record the names of something like fifty singers who took part in the oratorios during Handel's lifetime it is clear that some selection must be made. But wherever we look in the list we find a suggestiveness about the names which demonstrates how comprehensive eighteenth century music was. People specialized in being general, as someone has said of Mr Julian Huxley. In the early part of our period Carestini represents the hegemony

of the *castrato*; Strada and Cuzzoni show the transference of
loyalty from opera to oratorio; Francesina, for many years
devoted almost exclusively to the interests of Handel, added
a French influence to the cosmopolitan circle and graduated,
characteristically, to song by way of dance; Waltz was
reported to be a cook; Mrs Cibber was a versatile actress
and high in the lists of Shakespearean exponents; Mrs Clive
and Miss Brent proved that popularity at Vauxhall and
Ranelagh did not militate against fame in other and more
exacting fields; and then there was the faithful and charming
John Beard, in whom we find represented all the qualities—
and, if you like, the shortcomings—of English singers. The
upper work of the choruses was undertaken by choirboys
some of whom are proudly indicated in the scores as individuals. It was 'the boy' who sang the part of Damon in
the 1732 *Acis and Galatea* (his name, as we for once have it,
was Goodwill), some of the *Messiah* recitatives and arias
(according to the Dublin score), the parts of Joseph and
Benjamin, the air 'Happy Iphis' in *Jephtha*, and, particularly
effectively, ' 'Tis not Age's sullen face' and 'Chastity, thou
Cherub bright' in *Susanna*.

Behind the participation of choirboys was Bernard Gates,
one of the godfathers of English oratorio and happily placed
to lend active support to efficient choral collaboration
as he was both Master of the Choristers of the Chapel
Royal and also a member of the Abbey choir. Gates
himself sang in the performance of the *Dettingen Te Deum*
in 1743.

Audiences may have called for virtuosity and complained,
as they did, when deprived of it, but Handel—after many
years experience in handling the 'temperamental'—preferred
additional substantive qualities. He esteemed loyalty (and
one suspects that it was the affection and encouragement of
Francesina, Mrs Cibber, and Beard which at times kept him
to his projects) and intelligence. The latter point gives a
clue to interpretation. We may take some pride in the fact

that more often than not in the later days of his career it was the native singer who filled the role.

It will be recognized by anyone who has the slightest contact with a Handel score that to cope with almost any aria a complete singing technique is required. And if acquaintance starts with *Messiah* the reader may be reminded that the later oratorios are without much of the complexity, from the vocal aspect, of the early and more Italianate works. The eighteenth century was, of course, the age in which the technique of singing reached its zenith. Singers were the focal point; over their respective merits champions fought and argued as they do now over the equally debatable excellences of conductors. There is this difference. Singers served a rigorous apprenticeship and were quickly found out in imperfection, but less quickly forgiven. And yet Tosi, who must be our principal authority for the underlying principles of technique and style, could phrase disillusion in a sentence which has fathered a good many antithetical epigrams. 'He will be astonished at this bewildered Age, in which so many are paid so well for singing ill'.

At the outset it should be made clear that singers were accustomed to sing a good deal more than was put in the score. It was a period in which performance and composition were allied and not entirely disparate operations; if the performer was not, as frequently he was, a composer in his own right he was sufficiently acquainted with the theory of composition to be able to deal with the realization of figured bass and with melodic improvisation within the limits of free-style cadenza. A score was used as a shorthand version, or as a prompt copy, of a work which had been arranged in detail at rehearsal. One imagines that Francesina's divisions, which no doubt gave the appearance of spontaneity, were approved by Handel privately. But this *imprimatur* was not necessarily categoric: another singer with another style would be allowed different graces. The purist who labours at an authoritative edition can never come within measurable

distance of what was originally heard because of the high
degree of extemporization. At the same time we could re-
construct, hypothetically, scores which, with an overlay of
baroque ornament, would effectively disguise what we recognize as of Handel and which might give some idea of what
actually might have been heard.

The central feature of singing technique in the eighteenth
century was the bravura style. The more dextrous the quick-
flighted cadenza the greater was the impression made, although critical ears were early to complain of irrelevancies.
With regard to divisions in cadenzas Tosi picturesquely
observes that 'the Throat is set a going, like a Weather-cock
in a Whirlwind, and the orchestra yawns'. Elsewhere—'The
presumption of some Singers is not to be borne with, who
expect that an whole *Orchestra* should stop in the midst of a
well-regulated Movement, to wait for their ill-grounded
Caprices, learned by Heart, carried from one Theatre to
another, and perhaps stolen from some applauded female
Singer, who had better Luck, than Skill, and whose Errors
were excused in regard to her Sex.' These strictures might
be applied universally throughout the period for every singer
who was not Italian by birth became one (musically speaking)
by training; unless we except some of the English who were
more often than not disallowed the title of singer.

When one examines the examples quoted by Burney and
by Shield one may only conclude that vocal agility was
cultivated to an extraordinary degree, and after the commonplace roulades of lesser composers the dedication by Handel
of the bravura style to artistic ends becomes apparent, But
behind the artistry of Handel stood the technical accom-
plishment. The following:

74.
(a)

O

Sung by Visconti in Nerone (1753)

quoted by William Shield—
'Rudiments of Thorough
Bass', p. 81

demonstrate effectively the wide range of particular singers. There is plenty of evidence to suggest that quite fantastic feats were accomplished. With regard to competitive sopranos we may quote Burney:

De Amicis was not only the first who introduced *staccato divisions* in singing on our stage, but the first singer that I had ever heard go up to E flat in altissimo, with true, clear, and powerful *real* voice. The Agujari, long after, ascended much higher, but in falset. The Danzi, now Madam de Brun, went much higher than the Agujari, in *real* voice, of the same register as her middle notes . . . But I must own, that such tricks, such *cork-cutting* notes, as they were very well called by a musical lady of high rank, are unworthy of a great singer, and always give me more pain than pleasure.

We may conclude that Handel kept his voices within the

range of probability and eschewed the temptations laid before him by stratospheric sopranos.

In addition to agility and comprehensiveness of range there was the matter of expression and here we find the answer to the heresy that severe contrast, rather than graded change, is the invariable approach to dynamic problems. A singer, says Tosi, should be brought to 'swell by degrees from the softest *Piano* to the loudest *Forte*, and from thence with the same Art return from the *Forte* to the *Piano*'. Then there were the shakes to be mastered. 'Whoever has a fine shake, tho' wanting in every other Grace, always enjoys the Advantage of conducting himself without giving Distaste to the End or Cadence, where for the most part, it is very essential; and who wants it, or has it imperfectly, will never be a great Singer, let his Knowledge be ever so great.' There were shakes major, shakes minor, short shakes, rising shakes, descending shakes, slow shakes, redoubled shakes, shakes with a beat—and probably this list does not exhaust the possibilities. 'The shake to be beautiful, requires to be prepared, though on some Occasions, Time or Taste will not permit it. But in final Cadences, it is always necessary, now on the Tone, now on the *Semitone* above its Note, according to the Nature of the Composition.' Shakes come, says Tosi with some glibness, with practice, taste, and knowledge. Their use was at the discretion of the singer though it is remarked that there should be 'never too many, or too near one another; but very bad to begin with them' while certain kinds of composition were preserved from despoliation by custom: '*Divisions* and *Shakes* in a *Siciliana* are Faults, and *Glidings* and *Braggs* are Beauties.'

That the century knew rubato is apparent when Tosi complains on the one hand of the modern tendency to maltreat time and when, on the other, he comments: 'Ye stealing of Time, in the *Pathetick*, is an honourable Theft in one that sings better than others, provided he makes a Restitution with Ingenuity.'

Because most public singing was theatrical there was also
need for the singer to be something of an actor and it may
be considered as probable that the same sort of puppet
gesture which passed as effectively histrionic in opera went
also into oratorio, assuming, of course, that in the latter the
soloist was on the stage continuously. The presence in
Handel's casts of so many who were actresses first and
singers secondarily suggests that there may have been a good
deal in the way of dramatic convention. The rubrics in
Theodora, for example, probably received literal interpretation. In Scene V, Act II, Didimus 'at a distance, the visor of
his helmet closed' (which the audience read in their wordbooks) is instructed to approach Theodora. There follows
'Sweet rose and lily'. Then Theodora, 'starting' (which any
singer of sensitivity who lives the part must do involun-
tarily), 'Oh save me, Heaven'. The convention underlying
theatrical recitative is thus shown by Tosi. 'Being always
accompanied with Action . . . it cannot be beautiful, if not
expressed with that Decorum with which Princes speak, or
those who know how to speak to Princes.' As for church
recitative it 'requires some *Messa di Voce*, many *Appoggia-
tura's*, and a noble Majesty throughout'.

At the back of Handel's mind was this great and laborious-
ly constructed tradition of singing—a tradition which in
many essentials lasted at least until the time of Braham and
Pasta. Handel, moreover, was interested in singing so that
he was respected as a teacher of the art. Among his known
pupils was Frasi. Interested as he was, however, there were
certain considerations which made him avoid certain singers.
One amenable to friendly discipline was worth a good deal
to Handel, who appears to have been precise in regard to
interpretation, and argument with an intractable Cuzzoni or
Carestini took valuable time from rehearsal, time which
could ill be spared in view of the brief period available for
the copying of parts (orchestral and choral parts as well as
parts for the principals all had to be done and some by

Pl. VI.

View of the Gallery prepared for the reception of their Majesties, the Royal Family, Directors, & principal Personages in the Kingdom, at the COMMEMORATION of HANDEL in Westminster Abbey.

Interior of Westminster Abbey showing the Royal Box at the east end of the nave; during the Commemoration of 1784—after the engraving by E. F. Burney

Handel himself), individual and collective rehearsals, and the hundred and one business arrangements supervening. Therefore we come across names in the lists which carry little of the glamour attached to those opera singers who reduced the dignity of society ladies to impropriety and tattered disorder. Of the vagaries of opera stars Handel had had his fill in thirty years of opera management.

Two notabilities who temporarily accepted oratorio parts were Strada and Carestini; doubtless a summer engagement was more of an inducement than the prospect of being in at the establishment of a new art form. Montagnana should have been with them at Oxford in the July of 1734. Burney states that 'Handel's genius and fire never shine brighter than in the base songs which he composed for Boschi and Montagnana: as their voices were sufficiently powerful to penetrate through a multiplicity of instrumental parts, he set every engine at work in the orchestra, to enrich the harmony and enliven the movement'. However, Montagnana deserted Handel in 1734 for the operatic venture of the nobility and in his place was enlisted Waltz.

Strada was devoted to Handel. She was in the habit of going to parties with him, although the friendship gave some umbrage to her husband, and she refused to be cajoled to the opera by those of her colleagues who deserted to Lincoln's Inn Fields. She had this degree of uniqueness (in other respects she was also somewhat unique as her sobriquet 'The Pig' indicates). She was so willing to learn that the fact was remarked. Handel's friends 'used to say that by the care he took in composing for her, and his instructions, from a coarse singer with a fine voice, he rendered her equal at least to the first performer in Europe'. Her qualities were 'a fine and brilliant shake', a capacity to encompass 'passages of execution of a very agreeable and uncommon kind', a 'science and feeling' fit for the pathetic manner and, at the other end of the scale, some flair for comedy. In *Athaliah* Strada played Josabeth to Carestini's Joad.

The *castrato* succumbed to English morality. Consequently in oratorio the soprano and contralto parts increasingly become the province of women singers. In 1733, however, before oratorio had reached the environs of institutional religion, it was not thought outrageous to include a eunuch in the cast. Besides, Carestini had already played in *Deborah*. Quantz reminds us that Carestini—second only, perhaps, to Farinelli in English popular rating—was bold and felicitous in his ornaments, and that his soprano range was enormous. Burney adds to this that his original soprano (never heard in England) changed into the 'fullest, finest and strongest counter-tenor that has perhaps ever been heard'. Further he was 'a very animated and intelligent actor', possessed of 'a lively and inventive imagination'. Apart from the technique, the main impression derived from hearing a *castrato* would certainly have been one of power. The soprano of the *castrato* rivalled the brilliance and the weight of the complementary trumpet and one imagines that such a song as 'Let the bright Seraphim', although written after the cult had died and for a female singer, Signora Avolio, should have been the apogee for this type of singer. Further one imagines that with the decline of artificial voices the natural soprano tended to emulate her predecessor in frequent exhibitions of loud singing. The florid arias of Handel sounded, one must think, more virile in those days than now.

The Athaliah of the Oxford performance was Cecilia Young—she married Thomas Arne in 1736—and in her we find, after an interval of many years, an English singer competent to be compared with the Italians. She had been taught by an old friend of Handel—Francesco Geminiani, and is briefly noted as a high soprano 'with a good natural voice and fine shake'.

Cecilia Young was primarily a singer and only incidentally an actress. Her sister-in-law, Mrs Cibber (née Arne), who was introduced to oratorio in 1742, was best known as an actress. Of all Handel's friends Mrs Cibber must rank as one of the most fascinating. The public first came to hear of her as one of the principals in a *cause célèbre*. Her marriage, which had brought her great unhappiness, had all its lurid details laid out for public observation in the courts. The Arnes were a remarkably talented family and at the age of fourteen Susanna was performing at the little theatre in the Haymarket in her brother Thomas's *Tom Thumb*. Occasionally she was engaged to sing at concerts and in 1732 she appeared in Lampe's *Amelia* (text by Henry Carey)—*A New English Opera . . . After the Italian Manner*. So far the career is that of a singer, but in 1734 she married Theophilus Cibber, upon which her father-in-law, Colley Cibber, 'observed to his son, that though his wife's voice was very pleasing, and she had a good taste in music, yet as she could never arrive at more than the rank of a second-rate singer, her income would be extremely limited. The old man added that he had overheard her repeat a speech from a tragedy and he judged by her manner that her ear was good'. Mrs Cibber followed her father-in-law's opinions with respect in this matter, for few knew more than he about practical affairs in the theatre; she apprenticed herself to him as a pupil and rose to become one of the great actresses of her age. 'Her features, figure, and singing, made her appear the best *Ophelia* that appeared either before or since', wrote one admirer. 'Actresses may have had more majesty, more fire, but I believe that all the tragic characters, truly feminine, greatly conceived, and highly written, had a superior representative in Mrs Cibber than in any other actress', came from another. And at her death Garrick, to whom it is reported she had a strong facial resemblance, exclaimed— 'Then Tragedy is dead on one side'.

On her singing we may quote two opinions. Burney says briefly that she 'captivated every hearer of sensibility by her native sweetness of voice and powers of expression, as a singer'. Sheridan, the author of *British Education* (1769) had this to say:

No person of sensibility, who has had the good fortune to hear Mrs Cibber sing in the oratorio of *The Messiah*, will find it very difficult to give credit to accounts of the most wonderful effects of music produced from so powerful a union. And yet it was not by any extraordinary powers of voice (whereof she has but a moderate share), nor to a greater degree of skill in music (wherein many of the Italians must be allowed to exceed her), that she owed her excellence, but to expression only, her acknowledged superiority in which could proceed from nothing but skill in her own profession.

Add to what has already been said that Mrs Cibber was a persistent success as Polly Peachum (that she did a charity performance in December 1745 for the benefit of soldiers incapacitated in, or on leave from the continental wars gives her some claim to charitable interest), an adorable Juliet, and we see something of the versatility of the first contralto to sing the solos in *Messiah*.

Mrs Clive, born in 1711, was a year younger than Mrs Cibber and an actress of a different order. The keynote of Mrs Cibber, even in comedy, was dignity. Kitty Clive—so she was known while Mrs Cibber was always Mrs Cibber— 'was a mixture of combustibles: she was passionate, cross, vulgar, yet sensible, a very sensible woman, and as a comic actress of genuine worth—indeed, indeed she was a diamond of the first water'. What we know of her hardly argues a prima facie case for engaging her for oratorio.

> First giggling, plotting chambermaids arrive,
> Hoydens and romps led on by General Clive.
> In spite of outward blemishes she shone,
> For humour fam'd and humour all her own.
> Easy as if at home, the stage she trod,
> Nor sought the critic's praise, nor feared his rod.
> Original in spirit and in ease,
> She pleas'd by hiding all attempts to please.
> No comic actress ever yet could raise
> On humour's base more merit or more praise.

So she was defined by Charles Churchill. Dr Johnson

thought her—and this is incidentally interesting as showing something of his taste in actresses—the best player he ever saw. Horace Walpole, of whom Mrs Clive was a neighbour at Twickenham, likewise praised her in superlatives. Though she was so outstanding she was no blue-stocking; she spelt 'most audaciously'. Her singing was complementary to her acting, vulgar, full-bodied, continually probing for comedy (her mimicry of Mignotti brought the house down) and, if you enjoyed that sort of thing, in its way irresistible. Lydia Melford heard Mrs Clive at Vauxhall, where singers made a good living out of the performance of ballads, operatic and oratorio arias, but complained that 'her voice was so loud and so shrill, that it made my head ache through excess of pleasure'. Burney observed that 'her singing, which was intolerable when she meant it to be fine, in ballad farces and songs of humour was, like her comic acting, everything it should be'.

Such was the singer employed by Handel to sing Dalila in *Samson*. The personality of the singer is a clue to the interpretation of the part.

Horace Walpole thought hardly of the unconventional singers brought into the oratorio, as has already been noted. It was all very well for him to inveigh against the singers but Handel knew what he wanted: the fire of Mrs Clive, the self-possession of Mrs Cibber, the high intelligence of Beard and, again, his immense dramatic technique, the profundity of Savage and the brilliance of Signora Avolio for 'Let the bright seraphim'.

John Beard, more than any other singer, was the principal interpreter of Handel. As a boy at the Chapel Royal he had been inspired to devotion for Handel by Bernard Gates and he had sung in the 1732 performance of *Esther*. We next hear of him (his tenor voice must have settled down quickly) in the opera season of 1736-7: his performance in Galliard's *Royal Chace*—the hunting song 'With early horn' was a tenor's delight—called forth complimentary observation.

Next we find him in *Alexander's Feast, Acis and Galatea,* and
Atalanta. Thereafter his career was one of uninterrupted
success: the Handel oratorios on the one hand (the tenor
parts of the later oratorios were composed specially for
Beard) and farces and ballad operas on the other.

Charles Dibdin tells us what manner of singer Beard was.
His testimonial—and who could ask for a better unsolicited
recommendation?—reads:

I consider Beard, taken altogether, as the best English singer. He
was one of those you might fairly try by Shakespeare's speech to the
actors. He did not mouth it, but his words came trippingly from his
tongue; he did not out-Herod Herod, but he begot a temperance that
gave his exertions smoothness; he never outstepped the modesty of
nature, nor made the judicious grieve; in short, he never did more
than was set down for him; he never set on a quantity of barren
spectators to applaud while some necessary question of the song stood
still: he let his own discretion be his tutor, and held the mirror up to
nature . . . He was very valuable as an actor. In the *Jovial Crew, Love
in a Village, Comus,* and *Artaxerxes,* he gave proof of this in a degree
scarcely inferior to anybody.

Of Beard's private life we know this: that he scandalized
that exclusive branch of society represented most vocally by
Lady Mary Wortley Montague by marrying into the aristocracy in 1739, his wife being Lady Henrietta Herbert (née
Waldegrave); that he lived with her in great happiness until
her death in 1753; that in 1759 he married for the second
time. This wife was Charlotte Rich, daughter of the celebrated proprietor of Covent Garden Theatre. On the death
of old Rich in 1761 Beard became owner of the theatre.
Beard was one of those rare creatures of whom no man
spoke ill.

These were the most interesting among the singers who
assisted Handel in the performance of oratorio. But the list
may grow indefinitely and at the end we shall be left amazed
at the amount of money which must have been expended
on fees. Small wonder that so many ventures were commer-
cially unsound. Italian singers continued to appear, though

with less frequency as the years passed. *Castrati* came across from the opera every now and then—Guadagni, the friend of Garrick, Ricciarelli, and Guarducci being the most notable. The last of these passed some interesting observations on the attitude of the English and in his comments one reads the effectiveness of the ballad opera and the directness of Handel in destroying the former criteria. 'The English', he said, 'are such friends to the composer, and to simplicity that they like to hear a melody in its original state, undisguised by change or embellishment. Or if, when repeated, *rissioramenti* are necessary, the notes must be few and well selected, to be honoured with approbation.' Among the women were Frasi and Galli, both of whom were pupils of Handel. Galli achieved fame in 1746 by her interpretation of ''Tis Liberty' from *Judas Maccabaeus* and was encored every night. She went on singing for many years, appearing at Covent Garden as late as 1797. Late in life the once famous Cuzzoni was given, charitably, a *Messiah* engagement. Handel, friend and benefactor to 'decayed' musicians could not leave penury unrelieved; hence his kindly gesture to Cuzzoni in 1750.

The tradition of German basses was maintained by Thomas Reinhold. He, said by some to have been the natural son of the Archbishop of Dresden, arrived in London in 1731 and made his debut as Puzzletext, the fuddled chaplain of the *Grub-Street Opera*. From this he graduated to oratorio. He handed the authentic tradition of Handelian interpretation to his son, Frederick Charles, who was one of the singers in the Commemoration of 1784. Among the singers in *The Triumph of Time and Truth* in 1757 was a Mr Champness, who made a considerable reputation both in London and the provinces after Handel's death. He appears to be the only one whose career embraced at the one end the experience of singing under Handel's direction and at the other of taking part in the Commemoration.

Champness, together with Wass, the bass soloist in *Jephtha* represents a new species in the profession of singing—specialists in oratorio. Wass was a Gentleman of the Chapel Royal.

An oratorio cast was likely at any time to form a model for united nations in co-operation. The French, the Italians, the English, the Germans, and the Irish (to Mrs Clive should be added the name of Sullivan, an occasional bass) worked well together and the degree of goodwill between singers was noticeably higher at and after the middle of the century than earlier. The hero worship of expensive virtuosi—the more they were paid the more they tended to display ill manners—passed, and interest in oratorio was increasingly directed at the person of Handel himself and, by the discriminating, at the quality of the music.

In 1757 *Messiah* was performed for the first time at the Three Choirs Festival, the meeting that year being at Gloucester, and we find the London singers then—and for ever afterwards—making autumnal pilgrimage to the west country. Frasi, Wass, Beard, Miss Brent (the original Hamor of *Jephtha*), Champness, the Hon. Mrs Scott, sister to Mrs Arne (whose first husband was the composer Lampe) mingled with talented amateurs like the Rev Benjamin Mence and local lay clerks—of whom the most notable was Price of Gloucester—and choirboys, Charles Norris, a boy at Salisbury, appearing at one festival under the patronage of Handel's old friend James Harris, and all to do honour to one whom they remembered in his old age and whom they loved. Singers in England owed much to Handel. He, too, owed them something.

Chapter Thirteen

CONDITIONS OF PERFORMANCE

IT has been seen and it is, perhaps, generally realized that the operas and oratorios of Handel derived something of their character from the capacities of particular singers while, conversely, style in vocal performance and interpretation was influenced by the outlook of Handel. Singers, however, were not the whole of the story. There were also the more modest and probably not less gifted musicians who comprised the orchestra. The early eighteenth century orchestra has been allowed a good deal of abuse and disallowed the credit due to it in enlarging the emotional boundaries of music. The orchestra which Handel knew was the junction between the old and the new conceptions of the function of instrumental ensemble. The zest for colour—often overlooked because, acting on the classical-romantic antithesis, we reckon the Georgians somewhat vaguely as formalists—found one outlet in the enjoyment of novel demonstrations by enterprising horn-players, clarinettists, harpists, and percussion players. Handel was ever alive to modernity and he was conspicuous in involving new colour effects in his scores. Thus we discover that opportunities for colouring his scores, often in striking anticipation of the nineteenth and even the twentieth centuries, were avidly seized. His orchestral players were, therefore, as effective in collaboration as his singers.

Powell, the Welsh harpist, was included in the score of
Esther; in the same score the antique theorbo (lute) appears
for 'romantic' purpose; the opera *Tamerlano* uses clarinets—
an instrument which next appears as a rare entertainment
in Dublin and not again in the English orchestra until 1762;
violette marine (an invention of Signor Castrucci) came into
Orlando. In *Saul, Israel in Egypt* and in the alternative Dead
March in *Samson* there are trombones (even in 1784 Burney
complained of the difficulty of obtaining trombone players
for the Handel Commemoration), obtained from the 'Royal
Music' through the intervention of Valentine Snow, the
trumpet virtuoso who was sergeant trumpeter in the king's
service; especially effective kettle drums were borrowed
from the Tower for *Saul*; a carillon, to Jennens's discomfiture, enhanced the pageantry of the same oratorio;
Alexander Balus has a mandoline, *Semele* a side drum; Mr
Wich, the one horn player whose name has survived, had
his opportunities in *L'Allegro* and variously in brass ensemble passages with a colleague. The organ was frequently
used as ancillary to the colour texture and not merely as a
support to the chorus and in more than one oratorio two
organs appeared. The double bassoon, an instrument in the
manufacture of which Handel was personally interested,
came into *L'Allegro*. So much should be sufficient to impress
the sceptical that Handel was as alive to the possibilities of
the orchestra as any composer of later time.

Moreover there is the manner in which he used less
bizarre instruments. The solo oboe, the solo flute, the solo
bassoon, the solo trumpet was an index to emotional behaviour. By long association these instruments had defined,
or helped to define, particular situations. But Handel was
not content to rest on convention. Pianissimo trumpets,
with exquisite dramatic propriety, close 'Behold the listening
sun obeys' in *Joshua* and to parallel this there is the *da
lontano* effect in the angelic hymn in *Messiah*. The woodland
scene in *Alexander Balus* (Handel loved trees), 'Here, amidst

these shady woods' has muted violins and violas against pizzicati basses. The 'Pastoral Symphony' has violins divided into three, which is quite different from two violin and two viola parts, which the editors will substitute. In *Judas Maccabaeus* the wind hold their notes against the detached string chords which punctuate 'For Zion lamentation make'. The brass alone has appropriate comment for the Battle Symphony of *Saul*. At opposite ends of the emotional scale must be mentioned the cadaverous bassoon entry which evokes the spirit of Samuel in *Saul* and the erotic surround of Cleopatra's first aria in *Alexander Balus*. Here we have two flutes, violins and violas, divided cellos, pizzicati basses, harp and (as aforesaid) mandoline, while at the mention of 'subtle love' violins insert with arch insinuation an indicative triplet figure.

So far we have proceeded by way of the exceptional to show that Handel was no reactionary but it should not be supposed that the more normal methods of imbuing music with variety of colour were to be despised. Because there were fewer opportunities of winning respect by easy means the eighteenth century composer disposed his ideas often according to a subtle scheme which generally defeats our ear and our imagination. The prevalent instrumental form was the concerto grosso and the concerto grosso depended for its contrasts on the select body of solo players (two violins and cello) taking turns with the *ripieno* instruments. Berlioz, Elgar, and Falla, to take modern examples more or less at random, realized the charming possibilities of such variation but justice has not been done to Handel in the matter of his oratorio accompaniments where, after the pattern of the concerto grosso, he frequently left the voice supported by solo violin, cello, and harpsichord. The effect is delicious. More than this the oratorio is reduced at certain points to an intimacy which is both proper to the period and corrective to the pompous nineteenth century attitude which still prevails. To refer to *Messiah*, we have the opening of 'Comfort ye my people' presented without the *ripieno* instruments, which appear, quite climactically, at the fifth bar. 'Thus saith the Lord' may sound 'thin' without the *ripieno* but in compensation there is a more determined rhythmic bite and the soloist is allowed to concentrate on the dramatic possibilities of the recitative without being compelled to oversing. The aria, with its affinities with the fashionable solo cantata, becomes chamber music when properly accompanied and a new charm arises when, for example, violins, *senza rip*. embrace the transparent beauty of 'I know that my redeemer liveth'. Once again, as in the choruses, voices and instruments co-operate on equal terms and that, in any Handelian performance, is essential.

The numerical strength of Handel's orchestra depended on the accommodation of the theatre and, because oratorio was an offshoot from opera, its constitution was in general that of the theatre band. In the early part of Handel's career exact details are wanting but towards the end of the first half of the century they become available. We have these regarding a provincial orchestra—that employed at the theatre in Moon Street, Birmingham: organ, harpsichord, trumpet, bassoon, two cellos, two French horns, a pair of drums, six violins, and a tambourine. Clearly a matter here of cutting one's coat according to the cloth available. Oboes do not get a mention, which is surprising, while the omission of violas ('tenors' or even 'tenners' as they were called) is a commentary on the scarcity of those artistes. In 1759 at the Foundling Hospital they had for *Messiah* twelve violins, three violas, three cellos, two basses, four oboes, four bassoons, two horns, two trumpets, and drums. Four oboes and four bassoons seem to have been considered the ideal. To us it is an apparent extravagance. It should be remembered, however, that this reed ensemble was only employed in entirety in the choruses—and possibly in such items as the entry music for the Queen of Sheba where strings and wind discourse in dialogue after the seventeenth century manner of string and

wind consort dialogue. It should be remembered also that
unless there were a reasonable number of players the points
at which it was necessary to leave off from the violin parts
(which oboes more often than not doubled) to snatch a
hasty breath would be appallingly obvious! At Gloucester,
in 1757, they engaged 'three trumpets, drums, four hautboys,
four bassoons, two double-basses, violins, violoncellos, and
chorus singers in proportion'. In 1763, still at Gloucester,
there were 'sixteen treble violins, four tenors, four violoncellos, two double-basses, four hautboys, four bassoons,
two clarinets [this was after the London appearance of the
instrument in 1762], two French horns, three trumpets and
a pair of kettle drums'. In 1767 at St Philip's Church (now
the Cathedral) in Birmingham, *Messiah* was the culminating
feature of a three-day Handel festival, in which on Oct. 21
Samson and on the next day *Acis and Galatea* were given
in the King Street Theatre. The band had sixteen violins,
four violas, five cellos, two basses, four oboes, four bassoons,
two trumpets, two horns, and drums. The leader was the
well-known Malchair, a Rhinelander who settled in the Midlands, and the conductor Mr Capel Bond, the organist of
the churches of St Michael (the cathedral) and Holy
Trinity in Coventry. Bond had been giving oratorios in the
Midlands since the year of Handel's death, though it was
not until the ambitious scheme of 1767 that this form of
entertainment really came into its own in Birmingham. Of
the *Messiah* performance of that year we further learn that
the chorus numbered forty singers and the audience eight
hundred: an adequate choir for the period (although with
the development of the Three Choirs the tendency for increased size was becoming apparent) and of traditional proportion. The audience, too, was a good one.

The provincial spread of Handel's reputation and the
backwardness of Birmingham in catching up with other
towns is reflected in an effusive comment which found its
way into *The Gazette:*

P

In other Towns whilst Oratorios please
Shall we in gloomy silence spend our days?
Nor taste of those enjoyments that impart
Melodious sounds to captivate the heart?
Sons of Apollo who the name revere
Of Handel and his memory hold dear
Let not the circling season pass unsung;
And whilst you've power to charm the listening throng
Bid darkness fly, nor let it e'er be said
Where arts are cherished music droops its head.

It is probably fair to say that just as Handel improved the standard of singing so, by the opportunities which he offered them, he influenced the great strides which were made in orchestral technique. But there was one more revolution and this, in many ways, the most notable of all: the changed character of the audience which came to patronize Handel at the end of his life as compared with that which was attracted by him at the outset of his oratorio career. At first the audience was mainly fashionable and aristocratic; later it was much more heterogeneous and, if we may use the word, democratic. And this, perhaps, illustrates as well as anything else the manner in which Handel realized his English citizenship.

Esther, both in 1720 and 1732, was played to a select and private audience. By royal command, however, *Esther* was on May 2 transferred to the theatre in the Haymarket. The whole of the royal family were in attendance, the house was packed and five more performances followed. Unanimity in the royal family, a rare phenomenon, meant that the whole of society would inevitably be present. But taste was fickle in those years. *Deborah*, coming on top of the Handel-Bononcini rivalry and being subject to increased prices (boxes a guinea each and stalls half a guinea) was received with some reserve and, on account of the financial issue, some resentment.

What may be termed the middle period of Handel's

English career shows him endeavouring to compromise in some manner between the impulsive imperative of his own imagination and the presumed inclinations of his audiences. Organ concertos (that in B flat—Op. 4, No. 2 appears to have been particularly associated with *Esther*) afforded relief from severity; while *Israel in Egypt*, presented in company with the Funeral Anthem for Queen Caroline, suffered at its second performance the interpolation of a number of irrelevant Italian songs. However, nothing could save this oratorio. The very qualities which commend it to choral societies to-day were those which kept away the contemporary patron: unadulterated choral music was fitting for the church but not the opera house. Oratorio was primarily an entertainment. Its projected fourth performance had to be cancelled. It was Mr Walsh's habit to issue, after an oratorio performance, a book of the songs at the modest price of half-a-crown. Mr Walsh was an excellent man of business. He showed clearly the reaction to *Israel in Egypt* by not issuing his usual anthology. It was almost twenty years before this oratorio was heard again and altogether in the lifetime of the composer it had only nine performances.

In 1744, Mrs Delany pictured the metropolitan reaction to Handel. We have already mentioned the opposition from 'the fine ladies [those who were later to avoid the virtuous story of Theodora], petit maîtres, and *ignoramus's*'. Those who wanted diversion avoided the oratorio, but the faithful minority stood firm. 'All the opera people are enraged at Handel, but Lady Cobham, Lady Westmoreland, and Lady Chesterfield never fail it.' A little less than a month later the situation had however improved and Mrs Delany wrote to her sister more hopefully. 'The oratorios fill very well, notwithstanding the spite of the opera party; nine of the twelve are over.' But the later part of the year was unfortunate. Interest lapsed, subscription concerts were run at a loss and Handel fell ill. Then came a remarkable revival:

patriotism provoked a relieved public to see in Handel their spokesman and oratorios take on topical significance.

The last of the oratorios to meet with lukewarm support was *Theodora*. 'Never mind', said the composer to a commiserating friend, 'the music will sound better.' From 1750 onwards the story was one of unlimited enthusiasm and in the gallery we find the new audience of humbler pretensions.

Fielding in *Amelia* (1751) gives us this picture of the evening which Amelia and Mrs Ellison spent at Covent Garden. It was a Wednesday evening, Wednesdays and Fridays being the days set apart for oratorio ever since the Lord Chamberlain in 1737 had prohibited opera on those days during Lent.

. . . the two ladies went to the oratorio, and were there time enough to get a first row in the gallery. Indeed, there was only one person in the house when they came; for Amelia's inclinations, when she gave a loose to them, were pretty eager for this diversion, she being a great lover of music, and particularly of Mr Handel's compositions. Mrs Ellison was, I suppose, a great lover likewise of music, for she was the more impatient of the two; which was rather the more extraordinary, as these entertainments were not such novelties to her as they were to poor Amelia.

Though our ladies arrived full two hours before they saw the back of Mr Handel, yet this time of expectation did not hang extremely heavy on their hands; for, besides their own chat, they had the company of the gentleman whom they had found at their first arrival in the gallery, and who, though plainly, or rather roughly dressed, very luckily for the women, happened to be not only well-bred, but a person of very lively conversation. The gentleman, on his part, seemed highly charmed with Amelia, and in fact was so, for, though he restrained himself entirely within the rules of good breeding, yet was he in the highest degree officious to catch at every opportunity of showing his respect, and doing her little services. He procured her a book and wax-candle, and held the candle for her himself during the whole entertainment.

At the end of the oratorio he declared he would not leave the ladies till he had seen them safe into their chairs or coach; . . .

The reader must finish this story for himself, but there is some substance in Mrs Elizabeth Carter's complaint that

Interior of Westminster Abbey, showing the west (performing) end of the nave during the Commemoration—from a painting by Edward Edwards, A.R.A., exhibited at the Royal Academy, 1793

'profligate poor wretches, who lived inharmonious and dis-
orderly lives' patronized the oratorio. Not that profligacy
and poverty necessarily went together and Mrs Carter was
the last person to welcome any relaxation of the social
tradition that had formerly kept all but the wealthy outside
the opera house. At the same time to do Mrs Carter, one
of the earlier blue-stockings, credit it should be said that
she was quite defenceless against the 'powerful magic' of
Handel, whose music recalled to her 'fine passages from her
favourite authors, striking conversations, and the memory
of those she loved'.

We have on a number of occasions drawn attention to
the high general standard of musical intelligence in the eighteenth century. Music in the home was a lively factor in
promoting knowledge and the number of families who performed in ensemble is astonishingly large. There is a variety
of reasons to account for this phenomenon. A genuine love
for music, which fundamentally is an English characteristic;
a desire to move with the stream of fashion, the employment
and entertainment of artists at all times being one of the
tokens of social superiority; the effort to achieve cultural
ease, the period being one in which, in the higher circles,
learning was not disregarded for its own sake; sociability,
music having a good deal less rivalry than now from other
entertainments; the approach to female education, which
invited every young lady to learn the harpsichord; and, finally,
the dimensions of the Georgian residence. In an eighteenth
century house, even one of modest proportions, it was possible to accommodate a fairly complete orchestra. Thus it
was that Handel's rehearsals were domestic affairs. Either
at his own house, or at Carlton House, the residence of
Frederick, Prince of Wales or at his lodgings in Dublin, or
at Mrs Delany's, where Handel would call to play over his
sketches, or at Frasi's, it was possible to hear oratorios
taking shape.

Burney, as a young man, used to take every opportunity

of attending such rehearsals. Like many of Handel's devotees
he had developed his enthusiasm from boyhood, for Burney
was at school in Chester when Handel stayed there to rehearse *Messiah* and he had been present at that famous
rehearsal. In his *Sketch of the Life of Handel* Burney lifts the
formal curtain of history to show Handel as he really was
in rehearsal. It was his hospitable practice to entertain his
principals to dinner before rehearsal and when they got
down to work they were fortified with good food and excellent port. Sometimes misunderstandings arose from
faulty manuscript:

> At Frasi's, I remember, in the year 1748, he brought in his pocket
> the duet of *Judas Maccabaeus*, 'From these dread Scenes', in which she
> had not sung when the Oratorio was first performed in 1746. At the
> time he sat down to the harpsichord, to give her and me the time of it,
> while he sung her part, I hummed, at sight, the second over his
> shoulder; in which he encouraged me, by desiring that I would sing
> out—but unfortunately something went wrong, and HANDEL with
> his usual impetuosity grew violent: a circumstance very terrific to a
> young musician. At length, however, recovering from my fright, I
> ventured to say, that I fancied there was a mistake in the writing;
> which, upon examining HANDEL discovered to be the case: and then,
> instantly, with the greatest good humour and humility, said, 'I pec
> your barton—I am a very odd dog:—maishter Schmitt is to plame'.

This is charming, showing the sensitive musical nature impatient of slow apprehension of the music and, at the same
time, the rare courtesy which offers prompt and generous
apology. The memorable phrase in Burney's description is
'good humour and humility'.

Angry demonstration on the part of musicians is sometimes taken as a possibly pardonable sign of 'temperament';
less often is it regarded as the counterblast to discourtesy.
Handel was not infrequently irate, but, as the following
extract shows, he sometimes had good cause.

> . . . at the rehearsals of his Oratorios, at Carleton-House, if the
> prince and princess of Wales were not exact in coming into the Music-
> Room, he used to be very violent; yet, such was the reverence with
> which his Royal Highness treated him, that, admitting HANDEL to

have had cause of complaint, he has been heard to say, 'Indeed, it is cruel to have kept these poor people, meaning the performers, so long from their scholars, and other concerns'. But if the maids of honour, or any other female attendants talked, during the performance, I fear that our modern Timotheus, not only swore, but called names; yet, at such times, the princess of Wales, with her accustomed mildness and benignity, used to say, 'Hush! hush! HANDEL's in a passion'.

Which includes, I think, the most considerate comment ever made by Frederick, Prince of Wales, in the course of his stormy life. Such is the power of music.

The oratorio, as perfected by Handel in England, is, in some measure a tribute to the new middle class. Handel was himself essentially a member of this section of society, not only by reason of his vocation but also on account of his capacity for financial manipulation. The details of this I have related elsewhere, but it is important that Handel should be considered as a shrewd man of business. He had many friends among city tradesmen, brokers, civil servants, writers, dramatists, and actors and these friends formed the enduring part of his audience. The aristocracy, although among its members Handel also numbered some faithful friends, could follow its whims. By 1750 the people who patronized the oratorio were those who controlled civic and charitable affairs. This goes some way to explain why it was at that point that Handel pursued his course with stability and without the anxiety which had beset him in earlier life. By 1750 the middle class was conscious of the power which it had been acquiring throughout the century (and, indeed, for some long time before). A succession of wars had enabled contractors to grow wealthy on military requisitions, the port of London had expanded to meet the needs of departing armies and the increase of merchant shipping; education thrived on new wealth and while foundations had received enlarged endowments, new schools were called for to give opportunities to the children of many, who, having received minor attention in that respect, were concerned that the next generation should start life with fewer handicaps.

There were also more people engaged in the normal distri-
butive trades. A contemporary economist paints a picture
which indicates the near approach of Victorian prosperity.
The writer is also concerned, after the modern manner,
with the vast increase in non-productive, but remunerative
occupations.

> Such . . . are those of agents, factors, brokers, insurers, bankers,
> negotiators, discounters, subscribers, contractors, remitters, ticket-
> mongers, stock-jobbers, and of a great variety of other dealers in
> money, the names of whose employments were wholly unknown to
> our forefathers. As also are those of governors, directors, com-
> missioners, and of a vast train of secretaries, clerks, book-keepers and
> others, their attendants and dependants, most of which employs are
> peculiar to London, and are more lucrative than that of merchant
> exporter, and the profits of many of them must be vastly increased by
> the late great increase of the national debt.

These were the people who could afford to attend functions which, by the standard of general wage levels, were
expensive. An advertisement from *The Daily Advertiser* (17
February, 1743) gives the details of the first performance of
Samson:

> By subscription.—At the Theatre Royal in Covent Garden, to-
> morrow, the 18th inst., will be performed a new oratorio, called
> *Sampson* [*sic*]. Tickets will be delivered to subscribers (on paying their
> subscription money) at Mr Handel's house, in Brooke Street, near
> Hanover Square. Attendance will be given from nine o'clock in the
> morning till three in the afternoon. Pit and boxes to be put together,
> and no person to be admitted without tickets, which will be delivered
> that day at the office in Covent Garden Theatre, at half a guinea each;
> first gallery, 5s.; upper gallery, 3s. 6d. *Nota.*—Each subscriber is to
> pay six guineas upon taking out his subscription ticket, which entitles
> him to three box tickets every night of Mr Handel's first six per-
> formances in Lent. And if Mr Handel should have any more per-
> formances after the first six nights, each subscriber may continue on
> the same conditions.

There should be added to the cost of the seat in the theatre
the hire of coach or chair and the charge for programme.
The latter was indispensable. It supplied the words, which
with some of the foreign singers might quite well on

occasion have appeared obscure; the scene and the action; and those words which the poet had supplied and Handel had omitted from his setting. The wordbooks published for J. and R. Tonson were worth the shilling they cost if only for the excellence of the setting.

The cost of attendance at an oratorio may be set against some wage figures for the same period (i.e. *circa* 1750). The average for a labourer was ten shillings a week, for a printer as much, on occasion, as a guinea a week, for a journeyman engaged in framework knitting or stocking-weaving nine or ten shillings a week. It is small wonder that charity schools and foundling hospitals were necessary, that crime flourished, that prostitution was a popular profession, that in London people died of starvation. It is to the credit of the altruistic citizen of moderate means that he abhorred conditions which led to such conclusions and that he took steps in the direction of amelioration. Among the chief of English benefactors should be placed Handel whose music afforded material relief to thousands in his lifetime and spiritual relief to many more thousands after his death. Perhaps it is justice that that class which benefited from his charity in the first instance repaid the debt in the years to come by zeal in the preservation of his reputation.

Chapter Fourteen

CONCLUSION

ALL art is expressive of two points of view, those of the artist and his audience. In painting, poetry, the novel, the drama, the audience sees itself and either approves what it sees or disapproves. In music, and to a lesser extent in sculpture, the audience feels its own impulses: the representation of life is different from that experienced in the less intangible forms of expression but it is none the less real. In fact, being less tied to the wheels of seeming reality, music possesses in the greatest degree an inward perception of the motives of human thought. Thus music escapes a good deal of the trammelling influence of temporality; the emotional roots of behaviour are constant from generation to generation and when music enfolds these roots it does not matter whether it is ancient or modern. The exposition of the desire for belief in a higher power is equally evident in the great Masses of Palestrina, of Byrd, of Bach, of Beethoven, of Vaughan Williams and the fundamental statement of mingled faith and interrogation common to all those works strikes in the receptive mind an echoing chord. Therefore, substituting as may be desired the various emotions which prompt imaginative exploration and, accordingly, art, we feel the high cathartic function of music. We feel

A shaping and a sense of things beyond us
Great things and voices great.

Creative artists are finally judged not by the excellence of their technique, though skill in competent elucidation must always and as a matter of course be a part of greatness, but by their breadth of vision, their percipience in emotional diagnosis, their skill in spiritual therapeutics. Humanity in despair finds solace in music because music at once impresses man with his littleness and his greatness—his individual troubles hardly stir the life stream and yet his own spirit is an essential part, so he feels in the experience of music, of the spiritual macrocosm.

> *There's sure no passion in the human soul,*
> *But finds its food in music.*

So Lillo, who was contemporary with Handel, urges the personal while Addison, who was also contemporary with Handel, thus formally addressing the patron saint of music, speaks of the wider philosophical significance:

> *Music, the greatest good that mortals know,*
> *And all of heaven we have below.*

The supremacy of Handel consists of this; that he informs humanity about itself while pursuing at the same time the vision of the sublime. The pursuit of sublimity is an occupation unknown to the consciousness of the artist and that he follows it is in some part due to the environment in which he works. Which returns us to the point from which we started—the necessary co-operation of the audience.

Handel lived in the eighteenth century and was of that century. His life was that of an English citizen of the period. Handel was no eccentric, except in so far as we are all eccentrics, and his interest was in normality, so far as this state can be allowed existence. The oratorios were called into existence because society arrived by degrees at that stage where they became inevitable. We have seen how in the course of thirty years Handel changed the essence of his oratorios, though not the form. He exploited the diversionary, he allowed validity to the claim that the English language was fit for music, he picked from the sensitive mind of the forward poets the vision of landscape beauty, from the reforming preachers and the newly moralizing novelists a sense of didactic responsibility; he appreciated the tolerant foundations of English government and therefore exalted the conceptions of monarchy and Erastianism; he found human nature at its best in a disposition to large kindliness, and charity moved him to erect musical monuments equally imperishable with those of more material substance.

The intimacy of the oratorio with the period to which it historically belongs is increased when a further point, peculiar to music, is introduced. Music calls for sympathy between composer and audience; further it calls for sympathy between composer and his team of interpreters. Handel, as naturally will any self-respecting musician, sacrificed mere virtuosity if it entailed a predominance of irrelevant self-interest. His favourite singers could by no stretch of the imagination be regarded as the greatest of their generation, but they possessed attractiveness in their individual skill and a warm-hearted desire to contribute to a team effort.

The first aspect of the Handelian oratorio which we should see is that which reveals the character of the people for whom it was made. Most of the best of the English character, as it existed in the Georgian period, is distilled in the music of Handel. There are qualities which have, unfortunately, passed out of our nature. Hence the historian who looks at music may be forgiven for urging the importance of viewing a work of art in its natural setting, for only in this way will the essential virtues appear.

As age succeeds to age horizons narrow. We lose what was, unless the poet provokes our consciousness of the fact that the ultimate appreciation of excellence involves a realization of the wisdom of our ancestors. Broadmindedness is an attribute of the great and we are continually in danger of reading into facts what we imagine should be there. We adjust Shakespeare to our inclinations instead of the reverse, we make the Gothic classical and the classical Gothic, according to our generation, we revolutionize Mozart and revivify Bach. As for Handel we turn him this way and that, as an artist adjusts the position of his model, until he but faintly resembles himself. We even justify our actions.

When Handel died he was a popular institution. He was already the milch cow from which was drawn the means of sustenance for the sick and the indigent; his name was nationally acclaimed as a benefactor. He thus, unconsciously, became regarded as an ally of the more unfortunate members of society. Politics are often felt rather than expressed and, as the industrial revolution gave a voice to the hitherto mute, Handel was qualified on two accounts as a natural spokesman. He had proved his sympathy for the underdog. He had built the splendid and glorious vision of the heavenly Jerusalem in choruses (or rather in one chorus) which inspired the downtrodden with the ultimate hope of salvation. It is impossible to sing the 'Hallelujah' chorus without feeling an exhilaration. The exhilaration is, I believe, in this case physical but so contagious is it that the mind may easily be led into all sorts of immortal longings.

The celebrations in Westminster Abbey in 1784 showed that a new method of interpretation of Handel was possible. Hundreds of singers, together with hundreds of instrumentalists, could achieve prodigies of communal magniloquence. Then was set in motion the fallacy which contemplates physical vastness as an artistic quality. The lead was given to the nineteenth century. Choral societies of large proportions were founded, primarily to act as focal points for the new gregariousness of the industrial communities and to give pride and purpose to the developing social consciousness of such communities, and secondarily to commemorate Handel. There was, in truth, no music other than that of Handel which was technically within the comprehension of such

groups and of the works of Handel only a very few movements were possible.

Choirs grew larger and larger and festival succeeded
festival. The text of *Messiah* suited the puritanism of the
nineteenth century, for choral societies grew out of chapel
choirs and were for long supported by the influences of
nonconformity. As choirs increased in size so did orchestras
—hence the numerous attempts to 'improve' Handel's
orchestration.

Every multiplication of the choral singers, [writes Mr Capell] every
modern additional accompaniment and every liberty allowed the pre-
siding organist to fill the spaces with his turbid sounds is a departure
from Handel. A multiplication of singers makes for muzziness and
not an increase of power. The attempt is common nowadays to com-
pensate for this muzziness by providing an instrumental interest
foreign to Handel's intentions. . . .

And all this has come about through a native interest in
sociology and through a capacity for putting morality before
art and wishful thinking before pure philosophy. The
English are swayed by generous emotions and kindly prejudice overpowers the integrity of logic. We are forgetful,
romantic, and commonplace. Our music labours in consequence under a variety of handicaps. In an age when music
is affecting the community more than ever before it is
proper that we should follow the track of artistic truth.
Loose thinking in respect of art is dangerous and breeds a
contempt for precision in any form of mental behaviour.
Handel is the *summa summarum* of music to the vast majority
of those who count themselves as lovers of music. If this is
so we should endeavour to see Handel as he really is.

At a time when mass movements are irrepressible, when
the voice of the individual is rarely heard, when generosity
comes from Act of Parliament rather than from the charitable zeal of the citizen it is helpful to return to the finer
principles of the eighteenth century. When music suffers
(for music, as has been shown, not only directs but is directed
by the philosophy of the period in which it flourishes) from

the elephantine outlook, it is healthy that earlier standards of excellence should be recalled. Were we to appreciate the forgotten qualities of Handel—of charm, of humour, of athleticism, of verbal sensitivity—in singing his music we should be better educated. We should be gayer in outlook and that Handel would have desired. As the cult of Handel spread and the size of his intentions was magnified, so the person of Handel became more and more corpulent. Handel was once a young, attractive, and virile individual. In spirit he remained young.

In one particular we have retained one facet of the eighteenth century—cricket, which is obviously in spirit a magnificent example of what the Georgian gentleman thought. It is pre-eminently an opportunity for the individual to show his prowess. At the same time it is an activity which involves partial subordination of self. It is worth remembering that Handel could hardly have escaped being aware of this pastime. It was only three years after the composition of *Messiah* that Kent played against an all-England side. The engraving by Grignion after Francis Hayman shows a cricket match in progress at Mary-le-Bone Fields, in which Handel used frequently to walk. His friend and sometime patron, Frederick, Prince of Wales, was the first victim of bodyline bowling. He died from the blow of a cricket ball. We stand at this moment in danger of burdening our native game with unnatural severity. How much greater is the risk in relation to our art?

The lesson of Handel is this. That seriousness of philosophy can only arise from an ability to keep clear of sententiousness: that love of man for man is in itself evidence of the love of man for God: that music is the inspiration of independence. The Handelian oratorio is, if you like, sacred music: regard it with sanctity, but not sanctimony.

INDEX

INDEX

A

Avolio, Signora, 107, 113, 127, 210, 213

B

INDEX

This book is set in 12-point Monotype Garamond on 13-point body, a type-face originally cut by Jean Jannon at Sedan in 1621, and recut for the Monotype in 1926. This design was later ascribed to Claude Garamond when the Imprimerie Royale took over the punches in the XVII century.

Garamond is a light and elegant face, a feature particularly evident in its italic version. The italic capital letters differ in slope from the lower case letters, a characteristic of Garamond. The Monotype version differs from other revivals, the strokes are thinner, the capital A ends in a sharp upper point which lies slightly above other capital letters. As in many other type-faces of the time, the capitals are slightly lower than the ascenders, b, d, h, l and other letters.

The ornament used on the title-page comes from John Pine's " Horace", published in London in 1733.

Typography by Henry Jacob